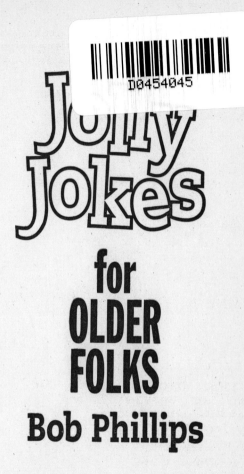

Jolly Jokes

for OLDER FOLKS

Bob Phillips

HARVEST HOUSE PUBLISHERS

EUGENE, OREGON

Cover by Dugan Design Group, Bloomington, Minnesota

Cover Illustration © Dugan Design Group

JOLLY JOKES FOR OLDER FOLKS
Copyright © 2007 by Bob Phillips
Published by Harvest House Publishers
Eugene, Oregon 97402

ISBN-13: 978-0-7369-2073-5
ISBN-10: 0-7369-2073-0

Printed in the United States of America

08 09 10 11 12 13 14 / RDM-SK / 14 13 12 11 10 9 8

A Baker's Job

A baker's job is a piece of cake. Of course, if it's a special job, he will rise to the occasion. It's the yeast he can do. Bakers trade bread recipes on a knead-to-know basis. But they stop making donuts when they get tired of the hole thing. In a bakery, buns usually play a small roll. But if you tell a baker his dough has fallen, you'll get a rise out of him. To find out how the business is doing, look at the pie chart. Old bakers never die. They just keep on making more dough.

A Good Pun Is Its Own Reword

A man's home is his castle—in a manor of speaking.

⊚ ⊚ ⊚ ⊚ ⊚

Dijon vu—the same mustard as before.

⊚ ⊚ ⊚ ⊚ ⊚

Sea captains don't like crew cuts.

🌀 🌀 🌀 🌀 🌀

Reading while sunbathing makes you well-red.

🌀 🌀 🌀 🌀 🌀

When two egotists meet, it's an I for an I.

🌀 🌀 🌀 🌀 🌀

A bicycle can't stand on its own because it is two-tired.

🌀 🌀 🌀 🌀 🌀

Time flies like an arrow. Fruit flies like a banana.

🌀 🌀 🌀 🌀 🌀

A backward poet writes inverse.

🌀 🌀 🌀 🌀 🌀

A chicken crossing the road is poultry in motion.

🌀 🌀 🌀 🌀 🌀

With her marriage, she got a new name and a dress.

🌀 🌀 🌀 🌀 🌀

Show me a piano falling down a mine shaft, and I'll show you a flat miner.

🌀 🌀 🌀 🌀 🌀

When a clock is hungry, it goes back four seconds.

◎ ◎ ◎ ◎ ◎

The man who fell into an upholstery machine is fully recovered.

◎ ◎ ◎ ◎ ◎

A grenade thrown into a kitchen in France would result in Linoleum Blownapart.

◎ ◎ ◎ ◎ ◎

You feel stuck with your debt if you can't budge it.

◎ ◎ ◎ ◎ ◎

Local Area Network in Australia: the LAN down under.

◎ ◎ ◎ ◎ ◎

He often broke into song because he couldn't find the key.

◎ ◎ ◎ ◎ ◎

Every calendar's days are numbered.

◎ ◎ ◎ ◎ ◎

A lot of money is tainted. It taint yours and it taint mine.

◎ ◎ ◎ ◎ ◎

A boiled egg in the morning is hard to beat.

@ @ @ @ @

He had a photographic memory that was never developed

@ @ @ @ @

A plateau is a high form of flattery.

@ @ @ @ @

The short fortune-teller who escaped from prison was a small medium at large.

@ @ @ @ @

Once you've seen one shopping center, you've seen a mall.

@ @ @ @ @

Those who jump off a Paris bridge are in Seine.

@ @ @ @ @

When an actress saw her first strands of gray hair, she thought she'd dye.

@ @ @ @ @

Santa's helpers are subordinate clauses.

@ @ @ @ @

Acupuncture is a jab well done.

◎　◎　◎　◎　◎

Marathon runners with bad footwear suffer the agony of defeat.

Abstract Art

Abstract art: a product of the untalented, sold by the unprincipled to the utterly bewildered.

Al Capp

Academic Whiz

A college basketball coach discovered a young high school prospect who was a dream come true. The youngster was 7'4" and never missed the basket. Unfortunately, he wasn't an academic whiz. The coach begged the academic dean to admit the young man. The academic dean agreed, saying, "I'll ask him three questions. If he answers them, he can be enrolled."

The young man was brought before the dean, who asked him the first question: "How much is two and two?"

Furrowing his brow, the young man thought and thought, finally saying, "Four."

The dean went on, "How much is four and four?"

The young man gulped, worked and worked, and finally said, "Eight."

The dean went on, "How much is eight and eight?"

Beads of sweat formed on the young man's forehead. After an eternity, he finally said, "Sixteen."

With that, the coach fell to his knees and said to the dean, "Give him one more chance!"

Actors

Q: How many actors does it take to change a light bulb?
A: Only one. They don't like to share the spotlight.

Acupuncturist

A patient calls his acupuncturist and says, "I have a terrible pain in my side."

The acupuncturist says, "Take two thumbtacks and call me in the morning."

Adam and Eve

Adam said to his wife, "Eve, I wear the plants in this family."

Adolescence

Adolescence is a kind of emotional seasickness. Both are funny, but only in retrospect.

Arthur Koestler

A Fool and His Money

A fool and his money are soon parted. One of the greatest puzzles is how the fool and his money got together in the first place.

Afterthought

Afterthought is the tardy sense of prudence that prompts one to try to shut his mouth about the time he has put his foot in it.

Agnostic

An agnostic is a person who says that he knows nothing about God, and, when you agree with him, he becomes angry.

Air Travel

My last flight was really no-frills. Instead of showing films, we just buzzed the drive-ins!

A Man of Few Words

A man stopped by the florist's to buy some flowers for his girlfriend.

"You want to say it with flowers, sir?" the florist asked. "How about three dozen American Beauty roses?"

"Make it half a dozen," the fellow said. "I'm a man of few words."

A Man-to-Man Talk

This broker took his young son aside, sat him on his knee, and said, "Son, let me tell you about the bulls and the bears."

Amazing

One fellow says, "In Florida they use alligators to make handbags."

His friend says, "Isn't it amazing what they can get animals to do?"

Amnesia

Never lend money. It gives people amnesia.

An Animal Tail

The minister was talking to the Sunday school class about kindness to animals and cited biblical references to substantiate his case.

"Now let's suppose," he said, "that you saw a bad person cutting off the tail of a cat. What biblical quotation would you use to tell him of the terrible wrong he was doing?"

One of the class members said, "I would remind him that 'what God has joined together, let man not separate.'"

Another Candle, Please

The waiter said, "Your dinner will be ariving shortly, sir. In the meantime, would you care for another candle?"

Antique

An antique is an object that has made a round-trip to the garage and back.

Ants

My wife made us a picnic lunch the other day. I felt sorry for the ants!

Apartment

An apartment is a place where you start to turn off your radio and discover you've been listening to your neighbor's.

Apathy

The number one problem in our country is apathy.. but who cares!

Appreciated

If you stand up, you'll be seen. If you speak up, you'll be heard. If you sit down, you'll be appreciated!

Argument

The only people who listen to both sides of an argument are the neighbors.

Armed

If a man with no arms has a gun, is he armed?

Astronauts

If astronauts are so smart, why do they count backward?

Atheist

An atheist was taking a walk through the woods. He said to himself, "What majestic trees! What powerful rivers! What beautiful animals!" As he was walking alongside the river, he heard a rustling in the bushes behind him. He turned to look. He saw a 7-foot grizzly charge toward him.

He ran as fast as he could up the path. He looked over his shoulder and saw that the bear was closing in on him. After looking over his shoulder again, he saw that the bear was drawing nearer. He tripped and fell on the ground, rolling over to pick himself up. But he saw the bear right on top of him, reaching for him with his left paw and raising his right paw to strike him.

At that instant the atheist cried out to God.

Time stopped.

The bear froze.

The forest was silent.

As a bright light shone upon the man, a voice came out of the sky: "You deny my existence for all of these years, teach others I don't exist, and even credit creation to a cosmic accident. Do you expect me to help you out of this predicament? Am I to count you as a believer?"

The atheist looked directly into the light, "It would be hypocritical of me to suddenly ask you to treat me as a Christian now, but perhaps could you make the *bear* a Christian?"

"Very well," said the voice.

The light went out.

The sounds of the forest resumed.

And then the bear dropped his right paw, brought both paws together, and bowed his head and spoke:

"Lord, bless this food, which I am about to receive from thy bounty. Amen."

Attention Deficit Disorder

Sound familiar to any of you? I have recently been diagnosed with A.A.A.D.D! Yikes! *Age Activated Attention Deficit Disorder.*

This is how it goes: I decide to wash the car; I start toward the garage and notice the mail on the table.

Okay, I'm going to wash the car. But first I'm going

through the mail. I lay the car keys down on the desk, discard the junk mail and I notice the trash can is full. OK, I'll just put the bills on my desk and take the trash can out, but since I'm going to be near the mailbox anyway, I'll pay these few bills first.

Now, where is my checkbook? Oops, there's only one check left. My extra checks are in my desk.

Oh, there's the Coke I was drinking. I'm going to look for those checks.

But first I need to put my Coke further away from the computer, or maybe I'll pop it into the fridge to keep it cold for a while.

I head toward the kitchen and my flowers catch my eye, they need some water. I set the Coke on the counter and— uh oh! There are my glasses. I was looking for them all morning! I'd better put them away first.

I fill a container with water and head for the flower pots—aaaaaagh!

Someone left the TV remote in the kitchen. We'll never think to look in the kitchen tonight when we want to watch television, so I'd better put it back in the family room where it belongs.

I splash some water into the pots and onto the floor, I throw the remote onto a soft cushion on the sofa and head back down the hall, trying to remember what I was going to do.

By the end of the day, the car isn't washed, the bills are unpaid, the Coke is sitting on the kitchen counter, the flowers are partially watered, the checkbook still only has one check in it, and I can't seem to find my car keys! When I try to figure out how come nothing got done today, I'm baffled because I know I was busy all day long!

I realize this is a serious condition and I'll get help, but first I think I'll check my e-mail.

Auctioneer

Old auctioneers never die. They just look forbidding.

Babies

Did you see the latest sign in the church nursery? It said, "All babies are subject to change without notice."

Baby

A man was complaining about the cost of the baby. The nurse said, "Sure, but look how long they last."

When you pick up a baby, everybody tells you to watch the head. That isn't the end that needs watching.

Bad Breath

A man goes to a dentist. During the examination, the man says, "My teeth are great. But let me tell you something. I never brush my teeth. I never use a rinse on my teeth. I never use a breath mint. I eat garlic all day long. And I've never had bad breath."

The dentist says, "You need an operation."

"On what?" Asks the man.

"On your nose."

Bad Luck

He's got no luck. He once put a seashell to his ear and got a busy signal.

Bad Potato

A diner in a restaurant called the waitress to his table. Pointing to a sad-looking baked potato on his plate, he said, "That potato is bad."

The waitress picked up the potato and slapped it roughly a couple of times. Then she put it back on the diner's plate.

"Now," she told the customer, "If that potato gives you any more trouble, you just let me know."

Bagel

Q: If a seagull flies over the sea, what flies over the bay?
A: A bagel.

Bagpipes

The best instrument is the bagpipes. They sound exactly the same when you have finished learning them as when you start.

Thomas Beecham

Bait

The cruelest thing you can hear on a party fishing boat: "That's a nice fish you caught. Can I use it for bait?"

Balanced Budget

Q: What is a balanced budget?

A: When money in the bank and the days of the month come out together.

Balance the Books

The boss comes in and asks a clerk, "Where's the accountant?"

The clerk says, "He's at the track."

"What's he doing at the track?"

"Trying to make the books balance."

Ballet

A little boy who went to the ballet for the first time with his father watched the girls dance around on their toes for a while, and then asked, "Why don't they just get taller girls?"

Bank Robbers

Two little girls were discussing the subject of piggy banks. "I think it's childish to save money that way," Mary said. "I do too," Annie replied. "and I also believe that it encourages children to become misers."

"And that's not the worst of it," Mary exclaimed. "It turns parents into bank robbers!"

Banks

Old bankers never die. They just lose interest.

I don't know how much I have in the bank. I haven't shaken it lately.

◎   ◎   ◎   ◎   ◎

Don't ever hit a bank loan officer in the heart. You'll break your hand.

◎   ◎   ◎   ◎   ◎

Savings and loans are closing by the hundreds today. If you want to rob one, make sure you call first to see if it's still open.

◎   ◎   ◎   ◎   ◎

Banks are really in trouble nowadays. I opened an account the other day, and I had to give *them* a toaster.

◎   ◎   ◎   ◎   ◎

My bank is in real trouble. I tried to make a withdrawal from an ATM, and an IOU came out.

◎   ◎   ◎   ◎   ◎

All banks are the same. They have one window at which ten people are standing. Then they have four windows called "Next Window."

Barber

The barber gave me a tonic and swore that my hair would grow in heavy. I now have one hair, but it weighs twelve pounds.

Beans

Visiting a parishioner's home for Sunday dinner, the minister placed some green beans on his plate.

Intently watching, the small daughter of the family suddenly exclaimed, "Look, Daddy, he took some beans! You said he didn't know beans!"

Beauty Spot

A woman went to the doctor's clutching the side of her face.

"What seems to be the problem?" asked the doctor.

"Well," said the woman, removing her hand, "it's this pimple on my cheek. A small tree is growing from it, along with a table, some chairs, and a picnic basket. What on earth can it be?"

"It's nothing to worry about," said the doctor, "It's only a beauty spot."

Bell Ringer

A church needed someone to ring the bell in the belfry on Sunday mornings. After advertising for the position, no one showed up except one young person without arms. The church administrator questioned his ability to ring the bell, but the young fellow proved that he could do it just by using his head. So one Sunday morning he overdid it, and he fell from the belfry and landed on the steps in front of the church. In viewing the body, a bypasser inquired who the person was. A member of the congregation responded, "I don't really know, but his face rings a bell."

Be Prepared

I am prepared to meet my Maker. Whether my Maker is prepared for the ordeal of meeting me is another matter.

Winston Churchill

Beverly Hills Widow

You can always tell when you see a Beverly Hills widow. She's wearing a black tennis outfit.

Big Liars

The two biggest liars in the world: the guest who keeps saying, "I must be going" and the host who asks, "What's your hurry?"

Bird Food

When churches seek a new incumbent, they expect him to have the strength of an eagle, the grace of a swan, the gentleness of a dove, the friendliness of a sparrow, and the night hours of an owl.

Then when they catch the bird, they expect him to live on the food of a canary.

Black and Blue

Ned: My wife is black and blue because she puts on cold cream, face cream, wrinkle cream, vanishing cream, hand cream, and skin cream every night.

Ted: Why should that make her black and blue?

Ned: She keeps slipping out of bed.

Blockhead

He's not merely a chip off the old block, but the old block itself.

Blonde

What do you get when a blonde dyes her hair? Artificial intelligence.

What does a blonde say when you blow in her ear? Thanks for the refill.

Blunder

Mark Twain was once asked the difference between a mistake and blunder. He explained it this way. "If you walk into a restaurant and walk out with someone's silk umbrella and leave your own cotton one, that is a mistake. But if you pick up someone's cotton umbrella and leave your own silk one, that's a blunder."

Bookkeepers

Old bookkeepers never die—they just lose their balance.

Boone Docs

First kid: Did you know that Daniel Boone's brothers were all famous doctors?

Second kid: No way.

First kid: Don't tell me you never heard of the Boone Docs?

Bowling

She joined the bowling team but quit. Her first ball knocked down four pins, but they wouldn't count it because they were in the next alley.

Braille

My latest book was so dull that they had to recall the Braille version. Blind people's fingers kept falling asleep.

Brains

John: How long can a man live without brains?
Russ: I don't know. How old are you?

Don: She's a bright girl...she has brains enough for two.
Art: Then she's just the girl for you.

Bride

Bride: The two best things I cook are meatloaf and apple dumplings.
Groom: Well, which is this?

Broken Heart

Pretty young girl to friend: Not only has Jack broken my heart and wrecked my whole life, but he has spoiled my entire evening!

Budget

A budget is a schedule for going into debt systematically.

Buffet Dinner

Buffet dinner: Where the hostess doesn't have enough chairs for everybody.

Buick Special

Their house specialty was Pollo con Riviera. That's a chicken that has been run over by a Buick.

Calculating

Any small child is capable of calculating that his tousled appearance at the height of a party will draw enough applause from the unmarried women present to win him at least half an hour out of bed and a biscuit.

Faith Hines

Cannibal

A cannibal returns home and tells his wife, "I just brought home an old friend for dinner."

The wife says, "Good. Put him in the freezer. We'll have him next week."

෧ ෧ ෧ ෧ ෧

"I don't like the look of the new missionary," said one cannibal to the other. "That's all right," said the other, "just eat the vegetables."

෧ ෧ ෧ ෧ ෧

There was an old cannibal whose stomach suffered from so many disorders that he could only digest animals that had no spines. Thus, for years, he subsisted only upon university professors.

Cannonball

The human cannonball decided to quit the circus. The owner was furious. "You can't quit!" he raged. "Where will I find another man of your caliber?"

Can You Hear Me?

The bishop was preaching his heart out but was concerned that because of the acoustics, people were finding it difficult to hear him. "Can you all hear me?" he stopped to ask. "I can," came a voice near the front, "but I don't mind exchanging with someone who can't."

Capital Punishment

Teacher: What is capital punishment?
Pupil (whose father is a businessman): It's when the government sets up business in competition with you and then takes all your profits with taxes to make up its loss.

Cartoons

There's too much violence on TV these days. The other day I saw two murders, six fights, an earthquake, and a nuclear disaster. That's the last time I'll watch the Saturday morning cartoons.

Catch of the Day

It's a great restaurant. Their catch of the day is fish sticks!

Change

The only time a woman really succeeds in changing a male is when he's a baby.

Jacob Braude

Cheating

The IRS recently received the following letter.

Dear Sirs:

Five years ago I cheated on my income tax, and recently it's been bothering me so much I can't sleep. Enclosed please find check for $35.00. If I still can't sleep, I'll send you some more.

Chewing Tobacco

"Why do rodeo cowboys chew tobacco?"
"To sweeten their breath."

Children

The trouble with your children is that when they're not being a lump in your throat, they're being a pain in your neck.

Child's View of Retirement

After a Christmas holiday break, the teacher asked her small pupils how they spent their holiday. One little boy's reply went like this: "We always spend Christmas at Grandma and Grandpa's.

"They used to live in a big brick house, but Grandpa got retarded, and they moved to Florida. They live in a park with a lot of other retarded people. They all go to a building they call the Wreck Hall, but it is all fixed. They all do exercises but not very well. They play a game with big checkers and push them around on the floor with sticks. There is a swimming pool, but I guess nobody teaches them—they just stand there in the water with their hats on. My Grandma used to bake cookies for me, but nobody cooks there. They all go out to restaurants that are fast and have discounts.

"When you come into the park, there is a doll house with a man sitting in it. He watches all day so they can't get out without him seeing them. I guess everybody forgets who they are because they all wear badges with their names on them.

"Grandma says that Grandpa worked hard all his life to earn his retardment. I wish they would move back home, but I guess the man in the doll house won't let them out."

Chill

A happily married man had only one complaint—his wife was always nursing sick birds.

One December evening, he came home to find a raven with a splint on its wing up on the fireplace mantel, a fevered eagle was pecking at an aspirin on the dining room table, and his wife was comforting a shivering wren that she had found in the snow.

Heaving a sigh, the man went to sit down in his favorite chair, only to discover a crow with a bandaged beak was already sitting there.

That was the last straw. He stormed furiously into the kitchen where his wife was wrapping the wren in a heated towel. "I've had it!" he cried, "We've got to get rid of all these blasted birds."

His wife cut him off. "Please dear," she hissed, "not in front of the chilled wren."

Christmas

One department store had two Santas during Christmas— one was an express line for kids who wanted nine toys or less.

They're planning to modernize the Christmas story. From now on, the three kings will bring gift certificates.

Chrysanthemum

A chrysanthemum by any other name would be easier to spell.

Church Absentee's Alphabet

I'd like to go to church but...

A is for auntie, who will come to tea,

B is for bed, which won't release me.

C is for car, "We need the fresh air,"

D is for dinner Mother must prepare.

E is for enthusiasm, which I haven't got,

F is for foursome, which golfs quite a lot.

G is for garden, much nearer God's heart,

H is for husband, who won't play his part.

I is for intruders, who sit in my pew,

J is for jealousy shown by a few.

K is for knitting which Mother likes so much,

L is for language, which is so out of touch.

M is for money, of which they always want more,

N is for new tunes we've never heard before.

O is for overtime, double on Sunday,

P is for preparing I must do on Monday.

Q is for queer noises, which come from the choir,

R is for rector, who ought to retire.

S is for sermons, as dull as can be,

T is for television I really must see.

U is for unfriendliness I always find,

V is for voices of the women behind.

W is for weather with too much rain or snow.

Y is for young rowdies, who sit at the back,

Z is for zeal—and that's what I lack.

Church Bulletin Bloopers

1. Scouts are saving aluminum cans, bottles, and other items to be recycled. Proceeds will be used to cripple children.

2. The outreach committee has enlisted 25 visitors to make calls on people who are not afflicted with any church.

3. The pastor would appreciate it if the ladies of the congregation would lend him their electric girdles for the pancake breakfast next Sunday morning.

4. The audience is asked to remain seated until the end of the recession.

5. Low Self-Esteem Support Group will meet Thursday at 7:00 to 8:30 PM. Please use the back door.

6. Ushers will eat latecomers.

7. The third verse of "Blessed Assurance" will be sung without musical accomplishment.

8. For those of you who have children and don't know it, we have a nursery downstairs.

9. The Rev. McArthur spoke briefly, much to the delight of the audience.

10. The pastor will preach his farewell message, after which the choir will sing, "Break Forth into Joy."

11. During the absence of our pastor, we enjoyed the rare privilege of hearing a good sermon when Reverend Lilley supplied our pulpit.

12. Next Sunday Mrs. Vernon will be soloist for the morning service. The pastor will then speak on "It's a Terrible Experience."

13. Due to the rector's illness, Wednesday's healing services will be discontinued until further notice.

14. Remember in prayer the many who are sick of our church and community.

15. The eighth-graders will be presenting Shakespeare's *Hamlet* in the church basement on Friday at 7:00 PM.

The congregation is invited to attend this tragedy.

16. The concert held in Fellowship Hall was a great success. Special thanks are due to the minister's daughter, who labored the whole evening at the piano, which as usual fell upon her.

17. Thirty members were present at the church meeting held at the home of Mrs. Swenson last evening. Mrs. Swenson and Mrs. Carlson sang a duet: "The Lord Knows Why."

18. On a church bulletin during the minister's illness: GOD IS GOOD—Dr. Poure is better.

19. Mrs. Huffman sang, "I Will Not Pass This Way Again," giving obvious pleasure to the congregation.

20. Ladies, don't forget the rummage sale. It is a good chance to get rid of those things not worth keeping around the house. Bring your husbands.

21. Next Sunday is the family hayride and bonfire at the Arnolds.' Bring your own hot dogs and guns. Friends are welcome! Everyone come for a fun time.

22. The rosebud on the altar this morning is to announce the birth of Paul Eric Simpson, the sin of Rev. and Mrs. Simpson.

23. This afternoon there will be a meeting in the South and North ends of the church. Children will be baptized at both ends.

24. Tuesday at 4:00 PM there will be an ice cream social. All ladies giving milk will please come early.

25. This being Easter Sunday, we will ask Mrs. Howell to come forward and lay an egg on the altar.

26. Next Sunday a special collection will be taken to defray the cost of the new carpet. All those wishing to do something on the new carpet will come forward and do so.

27. The ladies of the church have cast off clothing of every kind. They can be seen in the church basement Saturday.

28. The Senior Choir invites any member of the congregation who enjoys sinning to join the choir.

29. Weight Watchers will meet at 7:00 PM at the First Presbyterian Church. Please use the large double door at the side entrance.

30. Sign next to light in church bathroom: Beauty is only a light switch away.

31. Shane Walters and Erin Stratton were married on October 24 in the church. So ends a friendship that began in school days.

32. The church is glad to have with us today as our guest minister the Rev. Green who has Mrs. Green with him. After the service, we request that all remain in the sanctuary for the Hanging of the Greens.

33. Eight new choir robes are currently needed, due to the addition of several new members and to the deterioration of some of the older ones.

34. Please join us as we show our support for Anita and Mark in preparing for the girth of their first child.

35. The agenda was adopted...the minutes were approved...the financial secretary gave a grief report.

36. Barbara Van Verst remains in the hospital and needs blood donors for more transfusions. She is also having trouble sleeping and requests tapes of Pastor Hugo's sermons.

37. Announcement in a church bulletin for a National Prayer & Fasting Conference: "The cost for attending the Fasting & Prayer Conference includes meals."

38. Attend and you will hear an excellent speaker and heave a healthy lunch.

39. Applications are now being accepted for 2-year-old nursery workers.

40. Brother Lamar has gone on to be the Lord.

41. Don't miss this Saturday's exhibit by Christian Martian Arts.

42. Father, we just want to pray for our unloved saved ones.

43. Glory of God to all and peas to his people on earth.

44. If you are going to be hospitalized for an operation, contact the pastor. Special prayer also for those who are seriously sick by request.

45. In a show of near anonymity, the convention approved full communion with the Anglican Church of Canada.

46. Jean will be leading a weight-management series Wednesday nights. She's used the program herself and has been growing like crazy!

47. Lift up our Messianic brothers and sisters in Israel who are suffering during our prayer time.

48. Our next song is "Angels We Have Heard Get High."

49. Stewardship Offertory: "Jesus Paid It All"

50. The choir will meet at the Larsen house for fun and sinning.

51. The choir will sing "I Heard the Bills on Christmas Day."

52. The Honeymooners are now having bile studies each Tuesday evening at 7:30 PM.

53. The pastor will light his candle from the altar candles. The ushers will light their candle from the pastor's candle. The ushers will turn and light each worshiper in the first pew.

54. There will not be any Women Worth Watching this week.

55. We have received word of the sudden passing of Rev. Woodward this morning during the worship service. Now let's sing "Praise God from Whom All Blessings Flow."

56. Bertha Belch, a missionary from Africa, will be speaking tonight at Calvary Methodist. Come hear Bertha Belch all the way from Africa.

57. Please place your donation in the envelope along with the deceased person you want remembered.

58. The church will host an evening of fine dining, super entertainment, and gracious hostility.

59. We are always happy to have you sue our facility.

60. The activity will take place on the church barking lot.

61. Hymn: "I Am Thin, O Lord."

62. New Missionaries: Tim is a pilot and flies missionaries and supplies into the bush.

63. Volunteers are needed to spit up food at the food bank.

64. Head Deacon and Dead Deaconess nominations will be accepted at the next business meeting.

65. The visiting monster today is Rev. Jack Coleman.

66. Next Friday we will be serving hot gods for lunch.

67. If you would like to make a donation, fill out a form, enclose a check, and drip in the collection basket.

68. Newsletters are not being sent to absentees because of their weight.

69. Helpers are needed! Please sign up on the information sheep.

70. The District Duperintendent will be meeting with the church board.

71. As soon as the weather clears up, the men will have a goof outing.

72. Diana and Don request your presents at their wedding.

73. Lent is that period for preparing for Holy Weed and Easter.

74. For the Word of God is quick and powerful...piercing even to the dividing asunder of soup and spirit.

75. Glory to God in the highest, and on earth peach to men.

76. Child care provided with reservations.

77. Mark your calendars not to attend the church retreat.
78. I was hungry and you gave me something to eat; I was thirty and you gave me drink.
79. Praise the Lard!

Circulation

A teacher was giving a lesson on the circulation of blood. Trying to make the matter clearer, she said, "Now, class, If I stood on my head, my blood, as you know, would run into it, and I would turn red in the face."

"Yes," the class responded.

"Then why is it that while I am standing upright in the ordinary position the blood doesn't run into my feet?"

One little boy shouted, "'Cause your feet aren't empty!"

Class Reunion

A class reunion...where everyone gets together to see who is falling apart.

...a gathering where you come to the conclusion that most of the people your own age are a lot older than you are.

Clergy Parking Space

Sign outside of church: *Clergy Parking Space*
You park—You preach

Climbing Mountains

Mountain climbers say they climb mountains "because they're there." Somebody ought to let them know that that's the same reason most of us go around them.

Cold

It's been real cold. Yesterday I looked in my closet, and my coat was wearing a sweater.

Cold Cuts

What's good for cold cuts? Frozen Band-Aids.

College

My nephew made a deal with his parents. He asked them to give him the money it would cost to send him to college. They did, and he retired.

College Graduate

They have two children. The first is a college graduate, and the other one isn't working either.

Come On In

Little Billy, caught in mischief for the tenth time one day, was asked by his mother, "How do you expect to get into heaven?"

The lad thought a minute and replied: "Well, I'll just run in and out and keep slamming the door until St. Peter says: 'For heaven's sake, Billy, come in or stay out.'"

Community Fund

A community fund is an organization that puts all its begs into one askit.

Complaints

The Lord created the world in six days and rested on the seventh. On the eighth day, He started answering complaints.

Computers

Q: What is a computer's first sign of old age?
A: Loss of memory.

⊛ ⊛ ⊛ ⊛ ⊛

I'm so glad we have a six-year-old in the house. We needed somebody who understands computers.

⊛ ⊛ ⊛ ⊛ ⊛

If computers get too powerful, we can organize them into committees. That'll do them in.

Conductor

A viola player came home late at night to find police cars and fire trucks outside his house. The chief of police intercepted him.

"I'm afraid I have some terrible news for you," said the chief. "While you were out, the conductor came to your house, killed your family, and burned your house down."

The viola player was stunned. "You're kidding! The conductor came to my house?"

Conference

A conference is a long coffee break.

Congress

If the opposite of pro is con, does that make "congress" the opposite of "progress"?

Congressman

Congress loves to adjourn and go home. I can't understand it. If I was my congressman, I'd be afraid to go home.

Conscience

Too often when conscience tries to speak, the line seems too busy.

He won't listen to his conscience. He doesn't want advice from a total stranger.

Contribution

When he gives a check to charity, he doesn't sign it. He says he wants to keep his contribution anonymous.

Conversation

It's good to hold a conversation. Just let go of it once in a while.

Copyright

When you write copy, you own the right of copyright

to the copy you write, if the copy is right. If, however, your copy falls over, you must right your copy. If you write religious services, you write rite, and own the right of copyright to the rite you write.

Conservatives write Right copy, and own the right of copyright, to the Right copy they write. A right-wing cleric would write Right rite, and owns the right of copyright to the Right rite he has the right to write. His editor has the job of making the Right rite copy right before the copyright can be right.

Should Reverend Jim Wright decide to write Right rite, then Wright would write Right rite, to which Wright has the right of copyright. Duplicating his rite would be to copy Wright's Right rite, and violate copyright, to which Wright would have the right to right. Right?

Coroner

The following is an excerpt from a murder trial when the defense attorney was cross-examining the county coroner:

Attorney: Before you signed the death certificate, had you taken the pulse?

Coroner: No.

Attorney: Did you listen to the heart?

Coroner: No.

Attorney: Did you check for breathing?

Coroner: No.

Attorney: So, when you signed the death certificate, you weren't sure the man was dead, were you?

Coroner: Well, let me put it this way. The man's brain was

sitting in a jar on my desk. But I guess it's possible he could be out there practicing law somewhere.

Corporate Exercise Program

Exercise Calories burned per hour

Beating around the bush	75
Jumping to conclusions	100
Climbing the walls	150
Swallowing your pride	500
Passing the buck	25
Throwing your weight around depending on your weight	50-300
Dragging your heels	100
Pushing your luck	250
Making mountains out of molehills	500
Hitting the nail on the head	50
Wading through paperwork	300
Bending over backwards	75
Jumping on the bandwagon	200
Balancing the books	25
Running around in circles	350
Eating crow	225
Tooting your own horn	25
Climbing the ladder of success	750
Pulling out the stops	75
Adding fuel to the fire	160
Wrapping it up at the day's end	12

To which you may want to add your own favorite activities, including:

Opening a can of worms	50
Putting your foot in your mouth	300

Countdown

My wife turned 50 last year, and for her birthday dinner she arranged candles on the cake to form the numerals 5 and 0. This year the cake was decorated with a 4 and 9. "I've begun my countdown," she explained.

Credit

Why ask me to live within my income? I can't even live within my credit.

Crime & Politics

Q: What's the difference between crime and politics?
A: In crime, you take the money and run.

Criminal Justice

They're speeding up criminal justice in my hometown. They have a special court for people with eight crimes or less.

Crochet

Crocheting gives women something to think about when they are talking.

Crooked

At one time everybody thought the world was flat. Then they decided it was round. Today, we all know it's crooked.

Custer's Last Words

This is General Custer speaking. Men, don't take prisoners!

Customer Is Always Right

Store Manager: I saw you arguing with that customer who just left. I told you before that the customer is always right. Do you understand me?

Salesclerk: Yes, sir. The customer is always right.

Store Manager: That's better. Now what were you arguing with the customer about?

Salesclerk: Well, sir, he said you were an idiot.

Dallas Cowboys

Q: If there are three Dallas Cowboys riding in a car, who's driving?

A: The police.

Dangerous Food

Q: What is the most dangerous food to eat?

A: Wedding cake.

Dark Horse

The trouble with dark-horse candidates is you can't find out about their track record until you are saddled with them.

Darkness

If the speed of light is over 186,000 miles a second—what's the speed of darkness?

Dear God

Dear God,

Thank you for the baby brother, but what I asked for was a puppy. I never asked for anything before. You can look it up.

Liz

Dear God,

If we come back as somebody else, please don't let me be Marsha Dinkins—because her socks always fall down.

Lee Ann

Dear God,

Is it true my father won't get into heaven if he uses his golf words in the house?

Kimberly

Dear God,

I bet it's hard for you to love all of everybody in the whole world. There are only four people in our family, and I can never do it.

Brittany

Dear God,

Did you really mean it when you said, "Do unto others as they do unto you"? If you did, then I'm going to get even with my brother.

Olivia

Dear God,

My grandpa said you were around when he was a little boy. How far back do you go?

Alex

Dear God,

Did you mean for giraffes to look like that, or was it an accident?

Kelsey

Dear God,

In Bible times, did they really talk that fancy?

Jeremiah

Dear God,

What does it mean when it says that you are a jealous God? I thought you had everything you wanted.

Dustin

Dear God,

How come you did all those miracles in the old days and don't do any now?

Robert

Dear God,

Please send Steven to a different summer camp this year.

Douglas

Dear God,

Maybe Cain and Abel would not kill each other so much if they each had their own rooms. It works out okay with me and my brother.

Jimmy

Dear God,

I keep waiting for spring, but it hasn't come yet. What's up? Don't forget.

David

Dear God,

You don't have to worry about me. I always look both ways before I cross the street.

Jamie

Dear God,

I wish you would not make it so easy for people to come apart. I had to have 3 stitches and a shot.

Janet

Deception

Paul: She said I'm interesting, brave, and intelligent.

Bob: You should never go steady with a girl who deceives you from the very start.

Deep Questions

1. Why do you need a driver's license to buy liquor when you can't drink and drive?

2. Why isn't phonetic spelled the way it sounds?

3. Why are there interstate highways in Hawaii?

4. Why are there flotation devices under plane seats instead of parachutes?

5. Why are cigarettes sold in gas stations when smoking is prohibited there?

6. Do you need a silencer if you are going to shoot a mime?

7. Have you ever imagined a world with no hypothetical situations?

8. How does the guy who drives the snowplow get to work in the mornings?

9. If 7-Eleven is open 24 hours a day, 365 days a year, why are there locks on the doors?

10. If a cow laughed, would milk come out her nose?

11. If you tied buttered toast to the back of a cat and dropped it from a height, what would happen?

12. If you're in a vehicle going the speed of light, what happens when you turn on the headlights?

13. You know how most packages say "Open here"? What is the protocol if the package says, "Open somewhere else"?

14. Why do they put Braille dots on the keypad of the drive-up ATM?

15. Why do we drive on parkways and park on driveways?

16. Why is it that when you transport something by car, it's called a shipment, but when you transport something by ship, it's called cargo?

17. You know that little indestructible black box that is used on planes? Why can't they make the whole plane out of the same substance?

18. Why is it that when you're driving and looking for an address, you turn down the volume on the radio?

Deer

Did you hear about the guy whose girlfriend ran off with a tractor salesman and sent the poor sap a John Deere letter?

Q: What do you call a deer with no eyes?
A: No eye deer (no idea).

Delay

It's good to check in early at the airlines. That way, you learn about the delay faster.

Delicate Situation

My doctor has a real moral dilemma. Tomorrow he's operating on a malpractice attorney!

Dentist

A dentist is a person who runs a filling station.

Desk

A desk is a waste basket with drawers.

Diet

The second day of a diet is easier than the first. By the second day, you're off it.

Jackie Gleason

Diet: A selection of foods for people who are thick and tired of it.

Difference Between Men and Women

Let's say a guy named Fred is attracted to a woman named Martha. He asks her out to a movie, she accepts, and they have a pretty good time. A few nights later, he asks her out to dinner, and again they enjoy themselves. They continue to see each other regularly, and after a while, neither one of them is seeing anybody else.

But one evening, when they're driving home, a thought occurs to Martha, and, without really thinking, she says it aloud: "Do you realize that, as of tonight, we've been seeing each other for exactly six months?"

And then, there is silence in the car.

To Martha, it seems like a very loud silence. She thinks to herself: I wonder if it bothers him that I said that. Maybe he's been feeling confined by our relationship—maybe he thinks I'm trying to push him into some kind of obligation that he doesn't want or isn't sure of.

And Fred is thinking: Gosh. Six months.

And Martha is thinking: But, hey, I'm not so sure I want this kind of relationship either. Sometimes I wish I had a little more space, so I'd have time to think about whether I really want us to keep going the way we are—moving steadily toward, I mean—where are we going? Are we just going to keep seeing each other at this level of intimacy? Are we heading toward marriage? Toward children? Toward a lifetime together? Am I ready for that level of commitment? Do I really even know this person?

And Fred is thinking:…Wow—six months.

Different Drummer

Boss to employee: "You may march to a different drummer, but I want the beat to go faster."

Dilemma

What should you do if you see an endangered animal eating an endangered plant?

Diploma

Perhaps the best way to curb high school dropouts would be to make a high school diploma a prerequisite for obtaining a driver's license.

Diplomacy

Telling your boss he has an open mind instead of telling him he has holes in his head.

Diplomat

A diplomat is one who can yawn with his mouth closed.

Diplomats

How is the world ruled and how do wars start?

Diplomats tell lies to journalists and then believe what they read.

Karl Kraus

Directions

Did Moses wander in the wilderness because God was testing him, or do you think it was because, like most men, Moses refused to stop and ask for directions?

Director

I often feel like the director of a cemetery. I have a lot of people under me, but nobody listens!

General John Gavin

Dirty?

The restaurant I go to is closed on Mondays. That's when they do the dishes.

Disgust

If you've never seen a real, fully developed look of disgust, tell your son how you conducted yourself when you were a boy.

Kin Hubbard

Disk

Q: What happened when the computer fell on the floor?
A: It slipped a disk.

Divorce

One woman I know charged her husband with mental cruelty so severe it caused her to lose 30 pounds. "Divorce granted!" said the judge. "Oh, not yet," the woman pleaded. "First I want to lose another ten pounds."

Doctor

A doctor is a man who has his tonsils, adenoids, and appendix.

❂   ❂   ❂   ❂   ❂

Patient: Doctor, doctor! I keep thinking I'm a pair of curtains.
Doctor: For heaven's sake, woman! Pull yourself together!

❂   ❂   ❂   ❂   ❂

Patient: Doctor, doctor! I can't stop stealing things.
Doctor: Take these pills for a week. If they don't work, get me a color TV.

🌀 🌀 🌀 🌀 🌀

Doctor: Have your eyes been checked?
Patient: No, they've always been blue.

🌀 🌀 🌀 🌀 🌀

Patient: Doctor, doctor! I think I've swallowed a pillow.
Doctor: How do you feel?
Patient: A little down in the mouth.

🌀 🌀 🌀 🌀 🌀

Patient: Doctor, doctor! I think I'm shrinking.
Doctor: Well, you'll just have to be a little patient.

🌀 🌀 🌀 🌀 🌀

Patient: Am I getting better?
Doctor: I don't know. Let me feel your purse.

🌀 🌀 🌀 🌀 🌀

Doctor: (The doctor called Griff to let him know the results of his physical exam) Griff, I've got bad news and worse news. The bad news is that you have 24 hours to live.
Griff: Oh, no! That's bad, but what could possibly be worse that?
Doctor: I've been trying to get you since yesterday!

🌀 🌀 🌀 🌀 🌀

Patient: Doctor, doctor! How do I keep my ears from ringing?
Doctor: Get an unlisted head.

◎ ◎ ◎ ◎ ◎

Patient: Doctor, doctor, last night I dreamed I was a tepee. The night before, I dreamed I was a wigwam.
Doctor: Just relax—you're two tents.

◎ ◎ ◎ ◎ ◎

Patient: Doctor, doctor! I keep thinking I'm a bell.
Doctor: If the feeling persists, give me a ring.

◎ ◎ ◎ ◎ ◎

Patient: Doctor, doctor! I think I'm a chicken.
Doctor: How long has this been going on?
Patient: Ever since I was an egg.

◎ ◎ ◎ ◎ ◎

Patient: Doctor, doctor! I keep thinking I'm a clock.
Doctor: OK, relax. There's no need to get yourself wound up.

◎ ◎ ◎ ◎ ◎

Patient: Doctor, doctor! People keep ignoring me.
Doctor: Next!

◎ ◎ ◎ ◎ ◎

Patient: Doctor, doctor! I've only got 59 seconds to live.
Doctor: Wait a minute, please.

⊚ ⊚ ⊚ ⊚ ⊚

Patient: Doctor, doctor! My hair keeps falling out. What can you give me to keep it in?
Doctor: A shoebox. Next.

⊚ ⊚ ⊚ ⊚ ⊚

Patient: Doctor, doctor! I feel like a pack of cards.
Doctor: I'll deal with you later.

⊚ ⊚ ⊚ ⊚ ⊚

Wife: Thank you so much for making this house call to see my husband.
Doctor: Think nothing of it. There is another man in the neighborhood who is sick, and I thought I could kill two birds with one stone.

⊚ ⊚ ⊚ ⊚ ⊚

Q: How many doctors does it take to change a light bulb?
A: Depends on whether it has health insurance.

Doctor? I Used to Be a Doctor

I used to be a doctor,
   Now I am a health care provider.
I used to practice medicine,
   Now I function under a managed care system.
I used to have patients,
   Now I have a consumer list.
I used to diagnose,
   Now I am approved for one consultation.

I used to treat,
  Now I wait for authorization to provide care.
I used to cure patients,
  Now insurance carriers dare me not to cure them. If I do, I will use up my authorization and I could lose the patient.
I used to see patients on referral from doctors, patients, and friends,
  Now I must be listed in their Provider Manual.
I used to see patients who travel to see me,
  Now I am considered out of their approved geographic area.
I used to be paid a Usual, Customary and Reasonable (UCR) fee,
  Now I don't have a usual fee. Now there is nothing customary—only managed competition. Now who is reasonable?
I used to get paid,
  Now I accept the allowed charges as payment in full for covered services.
I used to be paid for professional services,
  Now I am not paid either for time, materials, or non-allowed services.
I used to be an independent specialist,
  Now I am a dependent ancillary care provider.
I used to provide charity care,
  Now since I am not an authorized provider, I am not permitted to provide charity, nor to barter, nor to offer advice.
I used to consider the insurance company as a third party carrier,

Now insurance is a fiscal intermediary between the provider and the consumer.

I used to care for my patients by appointment,
Now the patient requires authorization to make an appointment.

I used to provide hands-on care,
Now I provide hands-off, gloves-on procedures.

I used to use words to describe my care,
Now I must fill in all boxes with appropriate code numbers.

I used to provide necessary services,
Now I am unnecessary.

I used to have a front office coordinator,
Now triage is performed at the front line.

I used to have a clean office,
Now I am certified by the Occupational Safety and Health Administration (OSHA).

I used to have a practice,
Now I am employed to provide services.

I used to have a successful "people" practice,
Now I have a paper failure.

I used to spend time listening to my patients,
Now I spend time justifying myself to the authorities.

I used to have feelings,
Now I have an attitude. Now I don't know what I am.

The Former Doctor,
Harry F. Hlavac

Dogfish

The dogfish in Tennessee are big and mean. People report that they've seen two of them tree a bear.

Dog Food

Old Grouch: Give me two pounds of dog food now!
Salesclerk: Certainly, sir. Shall I wrap it up or will you eat it here?

Doggy Tunes

The parents were listening to their eight-year-old practicing away on his trumpet while their dog loudly howled at his side.

Finally, the father said: "Son, why don't you play something the dog doesn't know?"

Doing Well

My nephew brought home a report from school that said he was doing well for a six-year-old. The trouble is—he's twelve.

Dream

If people dream in color, is it a pigment of their imagination?

"In my dream last night, I dreamed you bought me a fur coat."
"When you dream tonight, wear it well."

Driving Your Friend Crazy

Want to drive a friend crazy? Send him a fax saying, "Disregard first fax."

Dull and Confusing

Good evening, ladies and gentlemen. You'll be glad to know that when I asked my secretary to type this sermon out for me, I asked her to eliminate anything that was dull or confusing. So in conclusion…

Education

Education is something you get when your folks send you to college. But it isn't complete until you've sent your own kids.

Eighty-Eight

Q: At 88 years of age, how do you feel when getting up in the morning?
A: Amazed!

Ludwig von Mises

Epitaph

Here lies the body
Of Jonathan Blake;
Stepped on the gas pedal
Instead of the brake.

This is the grave of Edmund Gray
Who died maintaining his right of way.
He was right—dead right—as he drove along,
But he's just as dead as if he'd been wrong.

Here lies the body of Charlotte Greer,
Whose mouth would stretch from Ear to ear.

🌀 🌀 🌀 🌀 🌀

Once I wasn't,
Then I was,
Now I ain't again.

🌀 🌀 🌀 🌀 🌀

Pardon me for not getting up (Ernest Hemingway's suggestion for his own epitaph).

🌀 🌀 🌀 🌀 🌀

Here lies Dr. Keene, the good Bishop of Chester,
Who ate up a fat goose, but could not digest her.

🌀 🌀 🌀 🌀 🌀

Here lies an honest lawyer—
That is Strange (Sir John Strange).

🌀 🌀 🌀 🌀 🌀

Here lies
Lester Moore
Four slugs from a 44
No Les
No More

🌀 🌀 🌀 🌀 🌀

My life's been hard
And all things show it;
I always thought so
And now I know it.

Owen Moore
Gone away
Owing more
Than he could pay

Here lies the body of our Anna
Done to death by a banana.
It wasn't the fruit that laid her low
But the skin of the thing that made her go.

Here I lie and no wonder I'm dead,
For the wheel of the wagon went over my head

Excuse my dust (Dorothy Parker's suggested epitaph).

The children of Israel wanted bread
And the Lord sent them manna;
Old clerk Wallace wanted a wife,
And the devil sent him Anna.

ⓢ ⓢ ⓢ ⓢ ⓢ

Here lies Johnny Yeast
Pardon me for not rising.

ⓢ ⓢ ⓢ ⓢ ⓢ

Here Lies
Ezekial Aikle
Aged 102.
The Good
Die Young.

ⓢ ⓢ ⓢ ⓢ ⓢ

Beneath this silent tomb is laid
A noisy antiquated maid;
Who from her cradle talked till death
And ne'er before was out of breath.

ⓢ ⓢ ⓢ ⓢ ⓢ

Here I lie bereft of breath
Because a cough carried me off;
Then a coffin they carried me off in.

ⓢ ⓢ ⓢ ⓢ ⓢ

Here snug in grave my wife doth lie,
Now she's at rest and so am I.

Exaggerate

Our next speaker is a fine man. It's hard to exaggerate
his accomplishments, but I'll do my best.

Exaggeration

Exaggeration is a billion times worse than understatement.

Excuse

The absent are never without fault, nor the present without excuse.

Benjamin Franklin

Executive's Slogan

If you don't have ulcers, you're not carrying your share of the load.

Face Lift

You know how you can tell whether a woman's had her face lifted? Every time she crosses her legs, her mouth snaps open.

Joan Rivers

Fair Pay

Grouch: I hear the football coach gets five times as much salary as the Greek professor. Isn't that quite a discrepancy?

Student: Oh, I dunno. Did you ever hear 40,000 people cheering a Greek recitation?

Family

Q: Why are families like a box of chocolates?
A: They're mostly sweet, with a few nuts.

Famous Predictions

"Computers in the future may weigh no more than 1.5 tons."

Popular Mechanics, *forecasting the relentless march of science, 1949*

❀ ❀ ❀ ❀ ❀

"I think there is a world market for maybe five computers."

Thomas Watson, chairman of IBM, 1943

❀ ❀ ❀ ❀ ❀

"I have traveled the length and breadth of this country and talked with the best people, and I can assure you that data processing is a fad that won't last out a year."

The editor in charge of business books for Prentice Hall, 1957

❀ ❀ ❀ ❀ ❀

"But what...is it good for?"

Engineer at the Advanced Computing Systems Division of IBM, commenting on the microchip, 1968

❀ ❀ ❀ ❀ ❀

"There is no reason anyone would want a computer in their home."

Ken Olson, president, chairman and founder of Digital Equipment Corp., 1977

✿ ✿ ✿ ✿ ✿

"This 'telephone' has too many shortcomings to be seriously considered as a means of communication. The device is inherently of no value to us."

Western Union internal memo, 1876

✿ ✿ ✿ ✿ ✿

"The concept is interesting and well-formed, but in order to earn better than a 'C,' the idea must be feasible."

A Yale University management professor in response to Fred Smith's paper proposing reliable overnight delivery service. Smith went on to found Federal Express

✿ ✿ ✿ ✿ ✿

"I'm just glad it'll be Clark Gable who's falling on his face and not Gary Cooper."

Gary Cooper on his decision not to take the leading role in Gone with the Wind

✿ ✿ ✿ ✿ ✿

"A cookie store is a bad idea. Besides, the market research reports say America likes crispy cookies, not soft and chewy cookies like you make."

Response to Debbie Fields' idea of starting Mrs. Fields Cookies

✿ ✿ ✿ ✿ ✿

"We don't like their sound, and guitar music is on the way out."

Decca Recording Co. rejecting the Beatles, 1962

"If I had thought about it, I wouldn't have done the experiment. The literature was full of examples that said you can't do this."

Spencer Silver on the work that led to the unique adhesives for 3M Post-it notepads

"So we went to Atari and said, 'Hey, we've got this amazing thing, even built with some of your parts, and what do you think about funding us? Or we'll give it to you. We just want to do it. Pay our salary, we'll come work for you.' And they said, 'No.' So then we went to Hewlett-Packard, and they said, 'Hey, we don't need you. You haven't got through college yet.'"

Apple Computer Inc. founder Steve Jobs on attempts to get Atari and H-P interested in his and Steve Wozniak's personal computer.

"Professor Goddard does not know the relation between action and reaction and the need to have something better than a vacuum against which to react. He seems to lack the basic knowledge ladled out daily in high schools."

New York Times editorial about Robert Goddard's revolutionary rocket work, 1921

"You want to have consistent and uniform muscle development across all of your muscles? It can't be done. It's just a fact of life. You just have to accept inconsistent muscle development as an unalterable condition of weight training."

Response to Arthur Jones, who solved the "unsolvable" problem by inventing Nautilus

🌀 🌀 🌀 🌀 🌀

"Stocks have reached what looks like a permanently high plateau."

Irving Fisher, Professor of Economics, Yale University, 1929

🌀 🌀 🌀 🌀 🌀

"Everything that can be invented has been invented."

Charles H. Duell, Commissioner, U.S. Office of Patents, 1899

🌀 🌀 🌀 🌀 🌀

"Louis Pasteur's theory of germs is ridiculous fiction."

Pierre Pachet, Professor of Physiology at Toulouse, 1872

🌀 🌀 🌀 🌀 🌀

"The abdomen, the chest, and the brain will be forever shut from the intrusion of the wise and humane surgeon."

Sir John Eric Ericksen, British surgeon, appointed Surgeon-Extraordinary to Queen Victoria, 1873

🌀 🌀 🌀 🌀 🌀

"640K ought to be enough for anybody."
Bill Gates, 1981

Famous Statements

It won't shrink in the wash.

🌀 🌀 🌀 🌀 🌀

You can put it together yourself in five minutes.

🌀 🌀 🌀 🌀 🌀

We'll only stay five minutes.

🌀 🌀 🌀 🌀 🌀

It's not the money, it's the principle of the thing.

🌀 🌀 🌀 🌀 🌀

Come on, tell me. I promise I won't get angry.

🌀 🌀 🌀 🌀 🌀

You don't need it in writing—you have my word.

🌀 🌀 🌀 🌀 🌀

I'll call you later.

🌀 🌀 🌀 🌀 🌀

Eat this—you'll like it.

🌀 🌀 🌀 🌀 🌀

We've had a lot of interest in this property.

🌀 🌀 🌀 🌀 🌀

I don't burn—I tan.

🌀 🌀 🌀 🌀 🌀

Your hair looks just fine.

🌀 🌀 🌀 🌀 🌀

I never inhaled.

🌀 🌀 🌀 🌀 🌀

You don't look a day over 40.

🌀 🌀 🌀 🌀 🌀

When it says empty, there's always a gallon or two left.

🌀 🌀 🌀 🌀 🌀

This'll be a short meeting.

🌀 🌀 🌀 🌀 🌀

Believe me, nobody'll dress up.

❀   ❀   ❀   ❀   ❀

Gimme a match, I think the gas tank is empty.

❀   ❀   ❀   ❀   ❀

That's not poison oak.

❀   ❀   ❀   ❀   ❀

We have plenty of room.

❀   ❀   ❀   ❀   ❀

Of course there's film in the camera.

❀   ❀   ❀   ❀   ❀

You can make it! That train isn't coming fast.

❀   ❀   ❀   ❀   ❀

They'll feel terrific once you break them in.

❀   ❀   ❀   ❀   ❀

Your table will be ready in five minutes.

❀   ❀   ❀   ❀   ❀

Why put the top up? It won't rain.

❀   ❀   ❀   ❀   ❀

We only had three days of rain here last summer.

But we can still be friends.

🌀 🌀 🌀 🌀 🌀

If it will make you happy, it will make me happy.

🌀 🌀 🌀 🌀 🌀

The check is in the mail.

🌀 🌀 🌀 🌀 🌀

It's supposed to make that noise.

🌀 🌀 🌀 🌀 🌀

I gave at the office.

🌀 🌀 🌀 🌀 🌀

This won't hurt.

🌀 🌀 🌀 🌀 🌀

Of course I love you.

🌀 🌀 🌀 🌀 🌀

The government will not raise taxes.

🌀 🌀 🌀 🌀 🌀

You never leave home without an umbrella.

🌀 🌀 🌀 🌀 🌀

My wife doesn't understand me.

@ @ @ @ @

The new ownership won't affect you—the company will remain the same.

@ @ @ @ @

Having a great time. Wish you were here.

@ @ @ @ @

Your insurance policy covers you for full replacement value.

@ @ @ @ @

The river never gets high enough to flood this property.

@ @ @ @ @

It was delicious, but I couldn't eat another bite.

Fat Chance

Why do "fat chance" and "slim chance" mean the same thing?

Fathers of 1900 and Today

In 1900, if a father put a roof over his family's head, he was a success. Today, it takes a roof, deck, pool, and 4-car garage. And that's just the vacation home.

In 1900, a father waited for the doctor to tell him when the baby arrived. Today, a father must wear a smock, know how to breathe, and make sure film is in the video camera.

In 1900, fathers passed on clothing to their sons. Today, kids wouldn't touch Dad's clothes if they were sliding naked down an icicle.

In 1900, fathers could count on children to join the family business. Today, fathers pray their kids will soon come home from college long enough to teach them how to work the computer and set the VCR.

In 1900, fathers pined for old country Romania, Italy, or Russia. Today, fathers pine for old country Hank Williams.

In 1900, fathers shook their children gently and whispered, "Wake up, it's time for school." Today, kids shake their fathers violently at 4 AM shouting: "Wake up, it's time for hockey practice."

In 1900, a father came home from work to find his wife and children at the supper table. Today, a father comes home to a note: "Jimmy's at baseball, Cindy's at gymnastics, I'm at gym, and the pizza's in the fridge."

In 1900, fathers and sons would have heart-to-heart conversations while fishing in a stream. Today, fathers pluck the headphones off their sons' ears and shout, "When you have a minute!"

In 1900, a father gave a pencil box for Christmas, and the kid was all smiles. Today, a father spends $800 at Toys 'R' Us, and the kid screams: "I wanted Sega!"

Favorite Songs of Bible Characters

Noah	Raindrops Keep Falling on My Head
Adam and Eve	Strangers in Paradise

Lazarus	The Second Time Around
Job	I've Got a Right to Sing the Blues
Moses	The Wanderer
Samson	Hair
Daniel	The Lion Sleeps Tonight
Joshua	Good Vibrations
Elijah	Up, Up and Away
Methuselah	Stayin' Alive

Fax

The store Santa said to the little girl, "And what would you like for Christmas?" The little girl said, "Didn't you get my fax?"

Feeling Better

Americans spent more money on doctors last year than ever before and it's working. More doctors are feeling better.

Fifteen Months

I'm sixty-five, but if there were fifteen months in every year, I'd only be forty-eight.

James Thurber

Fifty-Mile Hike

Men consider a fifty-mile hike physical fitness. Women call it shopping.

Fifty Thousand

For every person who dreams of making fifty thousand

dollars, a hundred people dream of being left fifty thousand dollars.

A. A. Milne

Fine Friend

He is a fine friend. He stabs you in the front.

Leonard Louis Levinson

Finished Speaker

I love a finished speaker,
I really, really do.
I don't mean one who is polished.
I just mean one who's through.

Bernard Brunsting

First Joke

A brunette, a redhead, and a blonde were on their way to heaven. God told them that the stairway to heaven was 1000 steps, and that on every 5th step He would tell them a joke. He told them not to laugh at any of the jokes along the way or else they would not be able to enter heaven.

The brunette went first and started laughing on the 45th step, so she could not enter heaven.

The redhead went next and started laughing on the 200th step, so she could not enter heaven either.

Then, it was the blonde's turn. When she got to the 999th step, she started laughing.

"Why are you laughing?" God asked. "I didn't tell a joke."

"I know," the blonde replied. "I just got the first joke."

Fishing

Two old codgers went fishing one morning. Sitting in the boat, neither of them said a word for hours. Then one shuffled his legs a little, trying to work out a cramp. He shuffled his legs again about two hours later. His buddy looked up and said, "Did you come to fish or to practice your dancing?"

Fishy Story

A family sat down to dinner with a guest at the table. Their young son said: "Mother, isn't this roast beef?"

"Yes, what of it?"

"Well, Daddy said he was bringing a big fish home tonight."

Five Dollars

When my nephew got into the Army, he had ten dollars to his name. Three years later, he came out and had five dollars. So the army can't be too bad. Where else can you live three years for five dollars?

Flies

You can catch more flies with honey than you can with vinegar. But who wants a lot of flies?

Fly

The good Lord didn't create anything without a purpose, but the fly comes close.

Football

Women will never play football. Imagine eleven women in public wearing the same outfit.

Forbes

Every morning I get up and look through the Forbes list of the richest people in America. If I'm not there, I go to work.

Robert Orben

Forbidden Fruit

Adam was but human—this explains it all. He did not want the apple for the apple's sake, he wanted it only because it was forbidden. The mistake was in not forbidding the serpent; then he would have eaten the serpent.

Mark Twain

Forgetful

My grandfather's a little forgetful, but he likes to give me advice. One day, he took me aside and left me there.

Ron Richards

Forget It

He planned to go on a vacation and forget everything. The first time he opened his suitcase, he discovered how nearly he had succeeded.

Forgiveness

An exasperated salesman abandoned his car in a no-parking zone and left this note:

"I've circled this block 20 times. I have an appointment and must keep it or lose my job. Forgive us our trespasses."

Upon returning, he found this note:

"I've circled this block 20 years. If I don't give you a ticket, I'll lose my job. Lead us not into temptation."

Fork in the Road

I got a puncture in a tire the other day. I didn't see the fork in the road.

French

I really impress people when I take my wife to dinner and order everything in French. The employees at McDonald's are amazed!

Friend

He's the kind of friend you can depend on. He's always around when he needs you.

Funeral

The number one fear in life is public speaking, and the number two fear is death. This means that if you go to a funeral, you're better off in the casket than giving the eulogy.

I can't understand why funeral processions are allowed to go through red lights. What's the hurry?

Genius

Every family should have at least three children. Then if one is a genius the other two can support him.

George Coote

George Washington

Father: Tell me, Susie, how did your test go today?
Susie: Well, I did just what George Washington did.
Father: How's that?
Susie: I went down in history.

Getting Married

- If Marilyn Monroe married Boutros-Boutos Ghali, then divorced him to marry Kenny G., she'd be Ghali G.

- If Jean Handy (SNL writer) married Andy Capp, then married Jack Paar, then moved on to Stephen King, she'd be Jean Handy Capp Paar King.

Guess Who?

The average family consists of 4.1 persons. You will have to guess as to who constitutes the .1 person.

Giving

When it comes to giving, some folks stop at nothing.

Going Home Early

A panhandler walked up to a nicely dressed man and asked: "Could you spare $5 for a poor unfortunate fellow?"

"Five dollars!" exclaimed the man. "Isn't that a bit steep to be to be asking for?"

"Well, yes," agreed the panhandler. "But I don't feel very well today and I would like to get my work done early so I can go home."

Golf

Sally: Elmer, why don't you play golf with Ted anymore?

Elmer: Would you play golf with a fellow who moved the ball with his foot when you weren't watching?

Sally: Well, no.

Elmer: And neither will Ted.

☺ ☺ ☺ ☺ ☺

I found a way of getting my doctor to make a house call. I bought a place on a golf course.

☺ ☺ ☺ ☺ ☺

An employee of the country club saw ex-president Gerald Ford stepping off the green and asked, "Do you notice anything different since you left office?"

"Yes," was the rueful answer. "A lot more golfers are beating me."

☺ ☺ ☺ ☺ ☺

I never kick my ball in the rough or improve my lie in a sand trap. For that I have a caddy.

Bob Hope

☺ ☺ ☺ ☺ ☺

After three sets and ten lessons, I finally got some fun out of golf. I quit.

☺ ☺ ☺ ☺ ☺

What goes putt-putt-putt-putt?
A bad golfer.

◎   ◎   ◎   ◎   ◎

"It's not that I really cheat," the golfer explained. "It's just that I play for my health, and the low score makes me feel better."

◎   ◎   ◎   ◎   ◎

A golfer set up his ball on the first tee, took a mighty swing, and hit his ball into a clump of trees.

He found his ball and saw an opening between two trees he thought he could hit through. Taking out his 3 wood, he took another mighty swing—the ball hit a tree, bounced back, hit him in the forehead, and killed him.

As he approached the gates of heaven, St. Peter saw him coming and asked, "Are you a good golfer?" to which the man replied, "Got here in two, didn't I?"

Golfer's Psalm

My golf clubs are my inequity;

I shall want them no more;

My driver maketh my ball to slice into green pastures;

My wedge causeth it to sink in still waters;

My mid-iron tempteth me, and I creep the fairway

To the sand trap for my ball's sake.

Yea, though I cross the creek in nine, I dubbeth my approach.

My putt runneth over.

My clubs and my balls maketh me to prepare a feast for my enemies, verily. I am their meal ticket.

Surely, I shall swing my clubs all the days of my life,

And I shall shooteth a hundred plus forever.

Good News / Bad News

The leader of the oarsmen in a Roman galley said to his men, "I have some good news and some bad news for you. The good news is that the captain said you can have the rest of the day off." When the cheers of the men died down, he went on, "You will also get an extra ration of bread tonight." As soon as that round of cheers ebbed, he went on, "The bad news is that tomorrow he wants to go water-skiing!"

A woman phoned her husband at work for a chat. "Sorry, darling," he said, "I'm really busy at the moment. I haven't got time to talk."

"Oh, this won't take long. It's just that I've got good news and bad news."

"Look," he repeated, "I really am busy. Just give me the good news."

"Well," she said, "the air bag works."

An artist went to the gallery that represented him. The owner said, "I have good news and bad news for you."

"What's the good news?"

"A man came in earlier today and asked me if your paintings would go up in price if you were dead. I told him that they would, so he bought all I had."

"What's the bad news?"

"He was your doctor."

Good Politician

You can always tell a good politician by the way he answers. He makes you forget the question.

Good Trade

Sally was driving home from one of her business trips in Northern Arizona when she saw an elderly Navajo woman walking on the side of the road. As the trip was a long and quiet one, she stopped the car and asked the Navajo woman if she would like a ride.

With a word or two of thanks, she got in the car.

After resuming the journey and a bit of small talk, the Navajo woman noticed a brown bag on the seat next to Sally.

"What's in the bag?" asked the woman.

Sally looked down at the brown bag and said, "It's a bottle of wine. I got it for my husband."

The Navajo woman was silent for a moment, and then, speaking with the quiet wisdom of an elder, said, "Good trade."

Gossip

Two women are lunching, and one looks off to see a

friend. She says, "Oh, there's Ruth. Do you believe that awful story about her?"

The other woman says, "Of course. What is it?"

◎　◎　◎　◎　◎

Q: What do they call someone who puts who and who together and gets wow!

A: A gossip.

Go to Sleep

In the middle of the night, a wife nudged her husband and said, "I can't sleep. I keep thinking there's a mouse under the bed."

Wearily, the husband said, "Start thinking there's a cat under the bed and go to sleep!"

Government Employees

"How many government employees does it take to screw in a light bulb?"

"Two. One to insist that it's being taken care of, and the other to screw it into a water faucet."

Grace

The bishop was the dinner guest. The table was beautifully prepared and the food looked delicious. They were ready to begin. The hostess spoke to her daughter, age six. "Mary, will you say grace, please." A rather long delay ensued. The mother coaxed the little girl, "Come on, Mary say what you heard me say this morning at breakfast." In a loud voice it came out, "O God, why ever did I invite that bishop to dinner tonight?"

Grammar

The 20 Basic Rules of English Spelling and Grammar
1. Be sure to never split an infinitive.

2. The difference between "teach" and "learn" should learn you to pay attention. Teachers don't have to pay attention, so they don't learn; they just teach.

3. Never use no double negative. There ain't no triple negative that ain't worse.

4. Always make a pronoun agree with their referent.

5. Many people love to use commas, which are not necessary. For instance, "She ate, the fool" is a comment. "She ate the fool" is correct, if she is a cannibal, you see.

6. One of the trickiest points in punctuation is to use apostrophe's correctly. They are as sensitive as measle's.

7. Never use "real" when you mean "very." Therefore: "She is real stupid" shows that you are very stupid. (This point is real important.)

8. Adjectives are not adverbs. Write careful. (I know that's hardly.)

9. Question marks can be dynamite. Use them carefully. "You sure are pretty?" means you are not sure I am pretty. That is an insult.

10. Many a student is undone by "who" and "whom." Remember George Ade's remark: " 'Whom are you?' she asked, for she had gone to night school."

11. Avoid the excessive use of exclamation points!!!! It is

silly to write, "Yesterday, I woke up!!!" because that suggests that today you did not, which is probably true.

12. When you want to say something that indicates anyone, or all of us, the pronoun "one" is better than "he" or "she." Fats Waller put it neatly: "One never knows, does one?"

13. Observe the difference between "don't" and "doesn't." It's shocking to hear so many high-school graduates say, "He don't care." What they mean, of course, is "I don't care." Their grades proved it.

14. Never write "heighth" or "weighth." They just are not righth.

15. If you write, "Who's hand is tapping my knee?" you'll never know who's pulling whose leg. Such information can be valuable.

16. "Irregardless" is not in the dictionary. "Hopefully" is—and I hope you never use it.

17. Don't use "neither" when you mean "either." Either use "neither" correctly or don't use it at all. And don't use "either" if you mean "ether" neither.

18. Guard against absurd and unnecessary repetitions. This here rule is especially important for new beginners.

19. A real booby trap to avoid is "when"—especially when a sentence like "I do not deny I wasn't afraid" occurs when you mean "I won't deny I was afraid."

20. Don't forget the crucial difference between "lie" and "lay."

a. The former takes no object ("I lie in bed") but the latter must ("Lay that pistol down, Mother").

b. "To lie" means to express something not true; "to lay" means expressing something more urgent.

Growing Old

I know I'm growing old. I use tenderizer in my Cream of Wheat.

You're an old timer if you can remember when movies were rated on how good they were, not on who was allowed to see them.

Remember when we used to laugh at old people when we were young? Do you recall what was so funny?

There's one advantage to being 102. There's no peer pressure.

Dennis Wolfberg

When we're young, we want to change the world. When we're old, we want to change the young.

❀ ❀ ❀ ❀ ❀

You know you're out of shape when you get out of breath playing chess.

❀ ❀ ❀ ❀ ❀

The years between fifty and seventy are the hardest. You are always asked to do things, and you are not yet decrepit enough to turn them down.

T.S. Eliot

❀ ❀ ❀ ❀ ❀

When she told me her age, I believed her—why not? She hasn't changed her story for five years.

❀ ❀ ❀ ❀ ❀

You know you're getting older when your birthday cake collapses from the weight of candles.

❀ ❀ ❀ ❀ ❀

You can tell you're getting older when you get into a heated argument about pension plans.

❀ ❀ ❀ ❀ ❀

You can tell you're getting older when a fortune-teller offers to read your face.

❀ ❀ ❀ ❀ ❀

The years that a woman subtracts from her age are not lost. They are added to the ages of other women.

Diane De Poitiers

🌀 🌀 🌀 🌀 🌀

Half-way

What do you get when you cross the Atlantic Ocean with the Titanic?
Halfway.

Halitosis

Mary Poppins moved to California and started a business telling people's fortunes. But she doesn't read palms or tea leaves, she smells a person's breath. The sign outside reads: "Super California Mystic, Expert Halitosis."

Hand Over the Keys

Son: Dad, the Bible says that if you don't let me have the car, you hate me.
Dad: Where does it say that?
Son: Proverbs 13:24. He that spareth the "rod" hateth his son.

Hans

Show me a woman who feeds her son Hans a big dinner...
and I'll show you a mother who has her Hans full!

Happiness

Happiness is learning your daughter's boyfriend has had his electric guitar repossessed.

Harvard Grad

How many Harvard grads does it take to change a light bulb? One. He grabs the bulb and waits for the world to revolve around him.

Headlines

"Drunk Gets Nine Months in Violin Case"

"Two Convicts Evade Noose: Jury Hung"

"Something Went Wrong in Jet Crash, Experts Say"

"Miners Refuse to Work After Death"

"New Study of Obesity Looks for Larger Test Group"

"Squad Helps Dog Bite Victim"

"Red Tape Holds Up New Bridge"

"Local High School Dropouts Cut in Half"

◎ ◎ ◎ ◎ ◎

"New Housing for Elderly Not Yet Dead"

◎ ◎ ◎ ◎ ◎

"Include Your Children When Baking Cookies"

◎ ◎ ◎ ◎ ◎

"Wild Wife League Will Meet Tonight"

◎ ◎ ◎ ◎ ◎

"Blind Woman Gets Kidney from Dad She Hasn't Seen in Years"

◎ ◎ ◎ ◎ ◎

"Arson Suspect Held in Massachusetts Fire"

◎ ◎ ◎ ◎ ◎

"Chef Throws His Heart into Helping Feed Needy"

◎ ◎ ◎ ◎ ◎

"Lucky Victim Was Stabbed Three Times"

◎ ◎ ◎ ◎ ◎

"Thugs Eat Then Rob Proprietor"

◎ ◎ ◎ ◎ ◎

"Man Is Fatally Slain"

@ @ @ @ @

"Stolen Painting Found by Tree"

@ @ @ @ @

"Grandmother of Eight Makes Hole in One"

@ @ @ @ @

"Pope Cites Dangers Facing the World: Names Eight Cardinals"

Heaven

If I ever reach heaven I expect to find three wonders there: first, to meet some I had not thought to see there; second, to miss some I had expected to see there; and third, the greatest wonder of all, to find myself there.

John Newton

Heavy Fun

Call dieters in the middle of the night, saying words like "Pastrami," "Cheese Cake," or "Banana Cream Pie."

Heimlich Maneuver

Customer: What's today's special?
Waiter: The Heimlich maneuver.

Helping Others

If it's true that we're here to help others, then what exactly are the others here for?

Hillbilly Mother Writing Her Son

Dear Son,

Just a few lines to let you know that I'm still alive. I'm writing this letter slowly because I know that you cannot read fast. You won't know the house when you come home...we've moved. I won't be able to send you the address as the last family that lived here took the number with them for their next house so they wouldn't have to change their address.

About your father...he has a lovely new job. He now has over 500 men under him. He is cutting the grass at the cemetery.

There was a washing machine in the new house when we moved in, but it isn't working too good. Last week I put 14 shirts into it, pulled the chain, and I haven't seen the shirts since.

Your sister Mary had a baby this morning. I haven't found out whether it is a boy or a girl, so I don't know whether you are an aunt or an uncle.

Your uncle Mario drowned last week in a vat of whiskey in a Dublin brewery. Some of his fellow workers dived in to save him, but he fought them off bravely. We cremated his body, and it took three days to put out the fire.

It only rained twice last week. First for three days, and then for four days. Monday it was so windy that one of our chickens laid the same egg four times.

We had a letter yesterday from the undertaker. He said if the last installment wasn't paid on your grandmother within 7 days, up she comes.

Your loving mother

P.S. I was going to send you $10.00, but I had already sealed the envelope.

Holding Our Own

The company was on maneuvers. After a two-hour march, one of the men asked the sergeant, "How far to the bivouac?"

"About three miles."

Another hour's march, and a second soldier asked, "How far to the bivouac?"

"About three miles."

An hour and a half went by, and a third soldier asked the same question. The response was the same, "Three miles."

A fourth soldier smiled and said, "Thank God we're holding our own."

Holy Scow

Parson David Maxwell bought a new boat and named it—well, what do you think? He named it "Holy Scow."

Homeless Turtle

Q: Why did the homeless turtle cross the road?
A: To get to the Shell station.

Honesty

"You have known the defendant how long?"

"Twelve years."

"Tell the court whether you think he is the type of man who would steal this money or not."

"How much was it?"

Honor

The louder he talked of his honor, the faster we counted our spoons.

Emerson

Hook, Line, and Sinker

A fisherman in a small boat sees another man get another small boat, open his tackle box, and take out a mirror. Curious, the fisherman asks what the mirror is for.

The other man says, "That's how I catch fish. I shine the sunlight on the water, fish come up to the top, and I nab them."

"Does that really work?"

"You bet it does."

"Well, I'll give you ten dollars for that mirror."

"Sure."

The transaction is completed. The fisherman says, "By the way, how many fish have you caught this week?"

"You're the sixth."

Host

You can always tell who the host is at a party. He's the one watching the clock.

Hostage

If someone with multiple personalities threatens to kill herself, is it considered a hostage situation?

Hot

In Oklahoma City, it got so hot and dry a few years ago that the Baptists were sprinkling, the Presbyterians were using a damp cloth, and the Episcopalians were giving rain checks.

Hot Stuff

At a church in Iowa City, where the town was caught in

one of those terribly hot summer spells, the minister said he would preach the shortest sermon of his career. It was just too hot to do a longer one. He sermonized: "If you think it's hot here in Iowa City...just you wait!"

How Many Church Members Does It Take to Change a Light Bulb?

Charismatic:

Only one.

Hands are already in the air.

Pentecostal:

Ten.

One to change the bulb, and nine to pray against the spirit of darkness.

Presbyterians:

None.

Lights will go on and off at predestined times.

Roman Catholic:

None.

Candles only.

Baptists:

At least fifteen.

One to change the light bulb, and three committees to approve the change and decide who brings the potato salad and fried chicken.

Episcopalians:

Three.

One to call the electrician, one to mix the drinks, and one to talk about how much better the old one was.

Mormons:

At least four.

Because of the importance of family, everyone needs to join in, including mom, dad, sister, and brother.

Unitarians:

We choose not to make a statement either in favor of or against the need for a light bulb. However, if in your own journey you have found that light bulbs work for you, that is fine. You are invited to write a poem or compose a modern dance about your light bulb traditions, including candescent, fluorescent, three-way, long-life, and tinted, all of which are equally valid paths to luminescence.

Methodists:

Undetermined.

Whether your light is bright, dull, or completely out, you are loved. You can be a light bulb, turnip bulb, or tulip bulb. Churchwide lighting service is planned for Sunday. Bring bulb of your choice and a covered dish.

Nazarene:

Six.

One woman to replace the bulb while five men review church lighting policy.

Lutherans:

None.

Lutherans don't believe in change.

Amish.

What's a light bulb?

Jewish:

Who needs bulbs? God said, "Let there be light."

How to Lose Weight

1. Try the garlic and limburger cheese diet...you don't lose any weight but you'll look thinner from a distance.

2. Go for the water diet—I had a friend who tried it—her husband lost 10 pounds and she (wife) gained 70 gallons. She drank 8 glasses of water a day for a month. The water went all the way down to her feet. For 3 months she walked around with wet feet. She even had to wear pumps.

3. With the 31 Flavors diet, you eat ice cream until your colon freezes.

Here are eleven steps to a lighter you:

1. Remove all clothing.

2. Trim finger- and toenails.

3. Shave legs, arms, head.

4. Clean wax from ears.

5. Brush teeth and use dental floss.

6. Remove lint from navel.

7. Sandpaper away all freckles.

8. Blot all perspiration.

9. Blow nose.

10. Empty your mind.

11. Exhale.

Now you can step on the scale. You're guaranteed to lose one pound!

How to Survive

Next Sunday Mrs. Brown will sing a solo at the morning service before the vicar preaches on the subject of "Terrible experiences and how to survive them."

Human

To err is human; to blame it on somebody else is even more human.

Hunch

I think his name was Quasimodo. I'm not sure, but I had a hunch.

Idiot

"You have the brain of an idiot."
"Want it back?"

Information

At a small desert gas station in the middle of nowhere,

there's a sign: *"Don't ask us for information. If we knew anything, we wouldn't be here."*

Ignorance

Ignorance is strange. It picks up confidence as it goes along.

Ignorant

Executive director: Your reports should be written in such a manner that even the most ignorant may understand them.

Assistant: Yes, sir. What part is it you don't understand?

I'm a Senior Citizen

- I'm the life of the party—even when it lasts until 8:00 PM.
- I'm very good at opening childproof caps with a hammer.
- I'm usually interested in going home before I get to where I'm going.
- I'm good on a trip for at least an hour without my aspirin, Beano, or antacid.
- I'm the first one to find the bathroom wherever I go.
- I'm awake many hours before my body allows me to get up.
- I'm smiling all the time because I can't hear a word you are saying.
- I'm very good at telling stories—over and over and over.

- I'm aware that other people's grandchildren are not as bright as mine.
- I'm so cared for—long-term care, eye care, private care, and dental care.
- I'm not grouchy, I just don't like traffic, waiting, crowds, children, politicians.
- I'm positive I did housework correctly before my mate retired.
- I'm sure everything I can't find is in a secure, safe place.
- I'm wrinkled, saggy and lumpy, and that's just my left leg.
- I'm having trouble remembering simple words like...
- I'm now spending more time with my pillows than with my mate.
- I'm anti-everything now—anti-fat, anti-smoke, anti-noise, anti-inflammatory.
- I'm realizing that aging is not for sissies.
- I'm walking more (to the bathroom) and enjoying it less.
- I'm going to reveal what goes on behind closed doors—absolutely nothing!
- I'm sure they are making adults much younger these days.
- I'm in the initial state of my golden years—SS, CD's, IRA's, AARP and so on.
- I'm wondering—if you're only as old as you feel,

how could I be alive at 150?

- I'm supporting all movements now—by eating bran, prunes, and raisins.

- I'm a walking storeroom of facts—I've just lost the storeroom.

- I'm a senior citizen, and I think I am having the time of my life.

Immature

You're only young once, but you can always be immature.

Dave Barry

Income Tax

An income tax return is like a girdle. If you put the wrong figure in it, you're apt to get pinched.

Individuality

A graduation ceremony is where the commencement speaker tells 2,000 students dressed in identical caps and gowns that individuality is the key to success.

Inexactitude

I'm not telling a lie. It's a terminological inexactitude.

Insanity

Insanity runs in my family. It practically gallops.

Cary Grant

Insight About Growing Older

Now that I'm getting older (but refuse to grow up), here's what I've discovered:

One—I started out with nothing, and I still have most of it.

Two—My wild oats have turned into prunes and All Bran.

Three—I finally got my head together; now my body is falling apart.

Four—Funny, I don't remember being absent minded...

Five—All reports are in; life is now officially unfair.

Six—If all is not lost, where is it?

Seven—It is easier to get older than it is to get wiser.

Eight—I wish the buck stopped here; I sure could use a few.

Nine—Kids in the backseat cause accidents.

Ten—It's hard to make a comeback when you haven't been anywhere.

Eleven—If God wanted me to touch my toes, He would have put them on my knees.

Twelve—When I'm finally holding all the cards, why does everyone decide to play chess?

Thirteen—It's not hard to meet expenses...they're everywhere.

Fourteen—These days, I spend a lot of time thinking

about the hereafter...I go somewhere to get something and then wonder what I'm here after.

Insomnia

Harry: How's your insomnia?
Larry: Worse. I can't even sleep when it's time to get up.

Insurance

"How many physicians does it take to change a light bulb?"
"That depends on the kind of insurance the bulb has."

David must have been the first insurance man. He gave Goliath a piece of the rock.

Internal Damage

"Hey Dad," one of my kids asked the other day. "What was your favorite fast food when you were growing up?"

"We didn't have fast food when I was growing up," I informed him. "All the food was slow."

"C'mon, seriously. Where did you eat?"

"It was a place called 'at home,'" I explained. "Grandma cooked every day and when Grandpa got home from work, we sat down together at the dining room table, and if I didn't like what she put on my plate, I was allowed to sit there until I did like it."

By this time, the kid was laughing so hard I was afraid he was going to suffer serious internal damage, so I didn't tell him the part about how I had to have permission to leave the table.

Internet Connection

Ten Ways You Know Your Internet Connection Is a Little Slow

1. Text on web pages is displayed as Morse code.

2. Graphics arrive via FedEx.

3. You believe a heavier string might improve your connection.

4. You post a message to your favorite newsgroup, and it displays a week later.

5. Your credit card expires while ordering online.

6. ESPN Web site exhibits "Heisman Trophy Winner"... for 1989.

7. You're still in the middle of downloading that popular new game—"PacMan."

8. Everyone you talk to on the 'net phone' sounds like Forrest Gump.

9. You receive e-mails with stamps on them.

10. When you click the "Send" button, a little door opens on the side of your monitor, and a pigeon flies out.

Interrupting

I don't mind you interrupting. Three heads are better than one.

In the Beginning

God created the heavens and the earth. Quickly He was faced with a class action lawsuit for failure to file an environmental impact statement.

He was granted a temporary permit for the project, but was stymied with the cease and desist order for the earthly part.

Appearing at the hearing, God was asked why He began His earthly project in the first place. He replied that He just liked to be creative.

Then God said, "Let there be light," and immediately the officials demanded to know how the light would be made. Would there be strip mining? What about thermal pollution? God was granted provisional permission to make light, assuming that no smoke would result from the ball of fire; that He would obtain a building permit; and to conserve energy, keeping the light off about half the time.

God agreed and said He would call the light "day" and the darkness "night." Officials replied that they were not interested in semantics.

God said, "Let the earth produce vegetation and plants bearing seed."

The Environmental Protection Agency agreed so long as native seed was used.

Then God said, "Let the waters bring forth creeping creatures having life; and the fowl that may fly over the earth." Officials pointed out this would require approval from the Department of Fish and Game coordinated with the Heavenly Wildlife Federation and the Audubongelic Society.

Everything was okay until God said He wanted to complete the project in six days. Officials said it would take at least 200 days to review the application and impact statements. After that there would be a series of public hearings. Then there would be 10 to 12 months before...

At this point, God created the other place!

Introduction

You have heard it said before that this man needs no introduction. Well, I have heard him, and he needs all the introduction he can get!

Invisible

Nurse: Doctor, there's an invisible man in the waiting room.

Doctor: Tell him I can't see him.

It's Great To Be a Man!

- Your last name stays put.
- The garage is all yours.
- Wedding plans take care of themselves.
- Chocolate is just another snack.
- Car mechanics tell you the truth.
- You don't care if someone doesn't notice your new haircut.
- Wrinkles add character.
- Wedding dress: $5000; tux rental: $100.
- The occasional well-rendered belch is practically expected.
- New shoes don't cut, blister, or mangle your feet.
- One mood, *all* the time.
- Phone conversations are over in 30 seconds flat.

- A five-day vacation requires only one suitcase.
- You can open all your own jars.
- You can leave the motel bed unmade.
- You can kill your own food.
- You get extra credit for the slightest act of thoughtfulness.
- Your underwear is $6.95 for a three-pack.
- If you are 34 and single, nobody notices.
- Everything on your face stays its original color.
- Three pairs of shoes are more than enough.
- You don't have to clean your apartment if the maid is coming.
- You don't mooch off others' desserts.
- You are not expected to know the names of more than five colors.
- You don't have to stop and think of which way to turn a nut on a bolt.
- You are unable to see wrinkles in your clothes.
- You don't have to shave below your neck.
- Your belly usually hides your big hips.
- Toilet seats can be left in their natural position—up.
- One wallet and one pair of shoes, one color, all seasons.
- You can "do" your nails with a pocketknife or your teeth.
- You have freedom of choice concerning growing a mustache.

- You never have to drive to another gas station because this one's just too icky looking.

- Christmas shopping can be accomplished for 25 relatives on December 24th in 45 minutes.

- You can quietly watch a game with your buddy for hours without ever thinking, "He's mad at me."

It's Later Than You Think

Everything is further than it used to be. I've given up running for my bus. It leaves faster than it used to. Seems to me they are making staircases steeper than they used to make them in the old days. And have you noticed the small print they are using? Newspapers are getting farther away when I hold them, and I have to squint to make out the news. No sense in asking to have them read aloud—everyone speaks in such a low voice that I hardly hear them.

The material in my suit is always too skimpy around the waist and the seat. Even people are changing—they are so much younger than they used to be when I was their age. On the other hand, people my own age are so much older than I am. I ran into an old classmate the other night and he had aged so he didn't recognize me. I got to thinking about the poor fellow while I was shaving this morning, and while doing so, I glanced at my reflection in the mirror. Confound it! They don't even make mirrors as good as they used to be!

It's Not Fair

Life isn't fair. The young don't know what to do, and the old can't do what they know.

It's Time to Go on a Diet When...

1. The man from Prudential offers you "group insurance."

2. You're standing on a corner in a red, white, and blue outfit...and when you yawn, strangers start to put letters in your mouth.

3. A buddy insists you rotate your shoes every 4,000 miles.

4. When you take a shower and find out that you have to let out the shower curtain.

5. When you are standing next to your car and get a ticket for double parking.

6. When you wear all white to a party and the host shows movies on you.

7. When your husband/wife puts a chalk mark on you to see where he/she hugged you last.

It Won't Last Forever

You're not yourself today. Enjoy it while you can.

Jehovah

Answering the door to two people who introduced themselves by saying, "Good morning, we're Jehovah's Witnesses," the white-bearded man replied, "Good, I'm Jehovah. How are we doing?"

J-O-B

Father: My son just received his B.A.

Neighbor: I suppose now he'll be looking for a Ph.D.
Father: No, now he's looking for a J-O-B.

Jogging

My doctor recently told me that jogging would add years to my life. I think he was right. I feel ten years older already.

Milton Berle

Joneses

Never keep up with the Joneses. Drag them down to your level.

I found out why it's so hard to keep up with the Joneses. They're on welfare.

Joys of Womanhood

- Women over 50 don't have babies because they would put them down and forget where they left them.

- One of life's mysteries is how a 2 pound box of candy can make a woman gain 5 lbs.

- My mind not only wanders, it sometime leaves completely.

- The best way to forget all your troubles is to wear tight shoes.

- The nice part about living in a small town is that when you don't know what you're doing, some-one else does.

- The older you get, the tougher it is to lose weight because by then, your body and your fat are really good friends.

- Just when I was getting used to yesterday, along came today.

- Sometimes I think I understand everything— then I regain consciousness.

- I gave up jogging for my health when my thighs kept rubbing together and catching my pantyhose on fire.

- Amazing! You hang something in your closet for a while and it shrinks two sizes!

- Skinny people irritate me! Especially when they say things like, "You know, sometimes I just forget to eat." Now I've forgotten my address, my mother's maiden name, and my keys. But I've never forgotten to eat. You have to be a special kind of stupid to forget to eat.

- A friend of mine confused her valium with her birth control pills. She had 14 kids, but she doesn't really care.

- I read this article that said the typical symptoms of stress are: eating too much, impulse buying, and driving too fast. Are they kidding? That is my idea of a perfect day.

- I know what Victoria's Secret is. The secret is that nobody older than 30 can fit into their stuff.

Jury Duty

Juries scare me. I don't want to put my faith in people who weren't smart enough to get out of jury duty.

Monica Piper

Just Listen

A store manager overheard a clerk saying to a customer, "No, ma'am, we haven't had any for some weeks now, and it doesn't look as if we'll be getting any soon."

Alarmed by what was being said, the manager rushed over to the customer who was walking out the door and said, "That isn't true, ma'am. Of course we'll have some soon. In fact, we placed an order for it a couple of weeks ago."

Then the manager drew the clerk aside and growled, "Never, never, never, never say we don't have something. If we don't have it, say we ordered it and it's on its way. Now, what was it she wanted?"

"Rain."

Kayak

Two Eskimos were paddling their kayak along the Alaskan coast. The temperatures were so freezing that even beneath their layers of clothing, the Eskimos started to feel the cold. In a desperate attempt to keep warm, they lit a fire, but the wooden kayak went up in flames, and the pair drowned. The moral of the story is that you can't have your kayak and heat it too.

Keep off the Grass

How do "Do Not Walk on the Grass" signs get there?

Killing Time

Does killing time damage eternity?

Kiss

A kiss is of no use to one, yet absolute bliss to two. The small boy gets it for nothing, the young man has to lie for it, and the old man has to buy it. It is the baby's right, the lover's privilege, and the hypocrite's mask. To a young girl, it is faith, to a married woman, it is hope, and to an old maid, it is charity.

Last Church Joke

"Did you hear my last church joke?"
"I certainly hope so."

Late Night Guest

Late-staying guest: Well, good night. I hope I have not kept you up too late.

Yawning host: Not at all. We would have been getting up soon, anyway.

Laugh

We are all here for a spell; get all the good laughs you can.

Will Rogers

He who laughs frightens away his problems.

◎ ◎ ◎ ◎ ◎

No man ever distinguished himself who could not bear to be laughed at.

Maria Edgeworth

◎ ◎ ◎ ◎ ◎

Laughter is a powerful force that keeps us from becoming a negative person.

R. E. Phillips

◎ ◎ ◎ ◎ ◎

The best way to cheer yourself up is to try to cheer somebody else up.

Mark Twain

◎ ◎ ◎ ◎ ◎

If you could choose one characteristic that would get you through life, choose a sense of humor.

Jennifer Jones

Lawyers

A client gets his bill from his lawyer and was stunned by the size of it. Furious, he called the lawyer and berated him for trying to squeeze him dry.

The lawyer listened for a while and then said, "You're such an ingrate. And to think that I named my boat after you."

◎ ◎ ◎ ◎ ◎

Lawyers should never ask a witness a question if they aren't prepared for the answer. In a trial, a Southern small town prosecuting attorney called his first witness, an elderly, grandmotherly woman to the stand.

He approached her and asked, "Mrs. Jones, do you know me?" She responded, "Why, yes, I know you, Mr. Williams. I've known you since you were a little boy, and frankly, you've been a big disappointment to me. You lie, you cheat on your wife, and you manipulate people and talk about them behind their backs. You think you're a big shot when you haven't the brains to realize you never will amount to anything more than a two-bit paper pusher. Yes, I know you." The lawyer was stunned!

Not knowing what else to do, he pointed across the room and asked, "Mrs. Jones, do you know the defense attorney?" She again replied, "Yes, I've known Mr. Bradley since he was a youngster too. He's a lazy, bigoted alcoholic. He can't build a normal relationship with anyone, and his law practice is one of the worst in the entire state. Not to mention that he cheated on his wife with three different women, and one of them was your wife. Yes, I know him."

The defense attorney almost died. Then the judge asked both counselors to approach the bench. With a stern face and in a very quiet voice, he said, "Listen! If either of you clowns asks her if she knows me, I'll throw you in jail for contempt."

Lethal Injections

Why do they sterilize the needles for lethal injections?

Let Me In

A woman arrived at the gates of heaven. While she was waiting for Saint Peter to greet her, she peeked through the gates. She saw a beautiful banquet table. Sitting all around were her parents and all the other people she had loved and who had died before her. They saw her and began calling greetings to her: "Hello—how are you!" "We've been waiting for you!" "Good to see you."

When Saint Peter came by, the woman said to him, "This is such a wonderful place! How do I get in?"

"You have to spell a word," Saint Peter told her.

"Which word?" The woman asked."

"Love."

The woman correctly spelled "love" and Saint Peter welcomed her into heaven. About a year later, Saint Peter came to the woman and asked her to watch the gates of heaven for him that day. While the woman was guarding the gates of heaven, her husband arrived. "I'm surprised to see you," the woman said. "How have you been?"

"Oh, I've been doing pretty well since you died," her husband told her. "I married the beautiful young nurse who took care of you while you were ill. And then I won the multistate lottery. I sold the little house you and I lived in and bought a huge mansion. And my new wife and I traveled all around the world. We were on vacation in Cancun, and I went water skiing today. I fell and hit my head, and here I am. What a bummer! How do I get in?"

"You have to spell a word," the woman told him.

"Which word?" Her husband asked.

"Czechoslovakia."

Little League

The coach talks it over with his Little Leaguers: "We have to use sportsmanship. No temper tantrums, no yelling at the umpire, and no being bad losers. Do you understand that?"

The kids nod.

The coach goes on, "Good. Now explain that to your mothers."

Loaned Books

Everything comes to him who waits. Except a loaned book.

Kin Hubbard

London

A guide, escorting a tour through a museum in London:
"The Egyptian mummy in front of you is over 5,000 years old. It's possible that Moses saw it."
Tourist: "Moses saw it? When was Moses ever in London?"

Long

Q: Do you know how long people should stay in a hospital bed?
A: The same way short people stay in their hospital beds.

Longevity

The secret to longevity is to keep breathing.

Sophie Tucker

Los Angeles

I love L.A. in the fall. I go outside, and I see the birds change color and drop out of the trees.

Lost

Last week, the luggage handlers at the airport were going to go out on strike, but they couldn't. Somebody lost the picket signs.

Make Up Your Mind

"I want to marry a smart woman, a good woman, a woman who'll make me happy."

"Make up your mind."

Marathon

There's a critical spot in marathon running. Just before you get to it, you're afraid you'll die. When you pass it, you're afraid you won't die!

Marblehead

Ken: In Massachusetts they named a town after you.
Bob: What is it?
Ken: Marblehead.

Magnetic

My wife is a magnetic woman. Everything she picks up, she charges.

Marriage and the Common Cold

How a typical husband responds when his wife comes down with a cold.

In the first year of marriage:

"Darling, I'm worried about my baby girl. You've got a bad sniffle, and there's no telling about these things with all the terrible viruses going around nowadays. I've called the emergency doctor, and I called your mother and she's coming to help with the cooking and cleaning."

In the second year of marriage:

"Listen, darling, I don't like the sound of that cough, I've made an appointment with the doctor. Now you go to bed like a good girl, and I'll take care of everything."

In the third year:

"Maybe you'd better lie down, darling. Nothing like a little rest when you're feeling lousy. I'll bring you something. Do we have any canned soup?"

In the fourth year:

"Now look dear, be sensible. After you feed the kids, do the dishes, and mop the floor, you better get some rest."

In the fifth year:

"Why don't you take a couple of aspirin?"

In the sixth year:

"If you'd just gargle or something, instead of sitting around barking like a seal all night..."

In the seventh year:

"For Pete's sake, stop sneezing! What are you trying to do, give me pneumonia?"

Married

A man in love is incomplete until he has married. Then he's finished.

Zsa Zsa Gabor

Matterhorn

From a schoolboy's exam paper: "Matterhorn was a horn blown by the ancients when anything was the matter."

Medical Help

"Doctor, I have trouble breathing."

"Don't worry. I'll give you something to stop that."

Meet the Burglar

In the middle of the night, a man comes down from the upstairs bedroom and finds a burglar halfway out the window.

The man says, "Don't panic. I'm not armed, and I won't call the police. I'd just like to bring my wife in to meet you because she's been hearing you downstairs for ten years."

Memory

The new loudspeaker system installed in the church has been given by Mr. Jones in memory of his wife.

Some people claimed that Reagan had a poor memory. At a press conference, a reporter said to the president, "You said that you would resign if your memory started to go."

Reagan laughed. "I don't remember saying that."

Mere Girl

The boy told his father he was second in his class, the top place being held by a girl.

"Surely, John," said the father, "you're not going to be beaten by a mere girl!"

"Well, you see," explained John, "girls aren't nearly as mere as they used to be."

Metric Cookies

Child: I'm making metric cookies.
Mom: What are you going to call them?
Child: Gram crackers.

Milkshake

After ordering a milkshake, a man had to leave his seat in the restaurant to use the rest room. Since he didn't want anyone to take his shake, he took a paper napkin, wrote on it, "The world's strongest weight lifter," and left it under his glass.

When he returned from making his call, the glass was empty. Under it was a new napkin with a note that said, "Thanks for the treat!" It was signed, "The world's fastest runner"

Million Dollars

The son of a real estate baron sits down to breakfast and

says, "Today I feel like a million dollars!"

His mother looks at him and says, "A million dollars? What makes you so depressed?"

Mistletoe

Some airlines are now putting mistletoe at the baggage counter. That way you can kiss your luggage goodbye.

Money

Workers earn it, spendthrifts burn it, bankers lend it, women spend it, forgers fake it, taxes take it, people save it, misers crave it, robbers seize it, rich increase it, gamblers lose it—we could use it.

Monogram Napkins

The restaurant even had monogrammed napkins. What class! At least I thought so until I saw my monogram crawl away.

More Sleep

Willie: Every morning I dream I'm falling from a 10-story building and just before I hit the ground, I wake up.

Wilma: That's terrible. What are you going to do about it?

Willie: I'm going to move into a 15-story building. I need more sleep.

Neat and Clean

I have a very neat doctor. He always washes his hands before he touches my wallet.

Nose Job

Patient: What would you charge to alter my nose?
Doctor: Five hundred dollars.
Patient: Anything cheaper?
Doctor: You can try walking into a telephone pole.

Nosy

My wife thinks I'm too nosy. At least that's what she writes in her diary.

Drake Sather

Not Enough

The child comes home from his first day at school.

His mother asks, "Well, what did you learn today?"

He replies, "Not enough. They want me back tomorrow."

Nothing

I love talking about nothing. It is the only thing I know anything about.

Oscar Wilde

Not My Fault

When my wife has an accident, it's never her fault. Two days ago, a building backed into her.

Not Too Bright

She's not too bright. I gave her a calendar watch. She nailed it to the wall.

He doesn't have all the lights on upstairs. He once froze in a drive-in because he went to see a movie called *Closed for Winter*.

Not Too Popular

He's not too popular. His answering machine hangs up on him.

Nuclear Scientists

"How many nuclear scientists does it take to screw in a light bulb?"

"Nine. One to screw it in, and eight to figure out what to do with the old one for the next twenty thousand years."

Nuts

On some trees it takes 5 years to produce nuts. But not the family tree.

Obedience

A permissive mother said to her wild little son, "Sit down and stop making so much noise."

"No, I won't...so there!" said the boy in an impudent tone.

"Stand up, then...I will be obeyed!"

Obsessive-Compulsive

I bought a book on obsessive-compulsive disorders. It's great. I've already read it 523 times.

Old

"Old" is when...Your friends compliment you on your new alligator shoes and you're barefoot.

"Old" is when..."getting a little action" means I don't need to take any fiber today.

"Old" is when..."getting lucky" means you find you car in the parking lot.

"Old" is when...an "all nighter" means not getting up to go to the bathroom.

Old Folks' Home

I am a hundred and two years of age. I have no worries since my youngest son went into an old folks' home.

Victoria Bedwell

Opera

The opera is a place where when a guy gets stabbed—he doesn't die—he just sings.

Opposites

Why are a wise man and a wise guy opposites?

Pane

Mr. Tweedy: I have a headache.

Mrs. Tweedy: Well, stick your head through the window.

Mr. Tweedy: How will that help?

Mrs. Tweedy: It will make the pane go away.

Sign in glass store:
We Cure Your Windowpanes.

Paranoid

"How many paranoids does it take to change a light bulb?"

"Why do you want to know?"

Parking

It's not so easy to get a parking ticket nowadays. First, you have to find a place to park.

Period

I found out why they call it period furniture. Your wife drags you into an antique store and says, "I want that! Period!"

Permanent Wave

A man was driving down the highway, and he saw a rabbit hopping across the road. He swerved to avoid hitting the rabbit, but unfortunately the rabbit jumped in front of the car and was hit.

The driver, being a sensitive man as well as an animal lover, pulled over to the side of the road, and got out to see what had become of the rabbit. Much to his dismay, it was dead. The driver felt so awful, he began to cry.

A woman driving down the same road came along, saw the man crying on the side of the road, and pulled over. She stepped out of her car and asked the man what was wrong.

"I feel terrible," he explained, "I accidentally hit this rabbit and killed it."

The woman told him not to worry; she knew what to do. She went to her car trunk, pulled out a spray can, walked over to the limp, dead rabbit, and sprayed the contents of the can onto the animal.

Miraculously the rabbit came to life, jumped up, waved its paw at the two humans, and hopped down the road. Fifty yards away, the rabbit stopped, turned around, waved again, hopped down the road another fifty yards, waved, and hopped another fifty yards.

The man was astonished. He couldn't figure out what substance could be in the woman's spray can! He ran over to the woman and demanded, "What was in your car? What did you spray on that rabbit?"

The woman turned the can around so that the man could read the label. It said: "Hair spray. Restores life to dead hair. Adds permanent wave."

Pessimist

Did you ever hear a pessimist count his blessings? Five, four, three, two...

If you are a complete pessimist, does it mean you are positively negative?

Pigs

Yes, and I have been sticking up for you. Someone said you aren't fit to live with pigs, and I said you were.

Playpen

When my kids become wild and unruly, I use a nice safe playpen. When they're finished, I climb out.

Erma Bombeck

Political Career

He knows nothing and thinks he knows everything. That points clearly to a political career.

@ @ @ @ @

Politicians didn't invent crime. They just improved on it.

Pope's Visit To Texas

On a tour of Texas, the Pope took a couple of days off his itinerary to visit the Texas coastline on an impromptu sightseeing trip. His 4x4 Pope mobile was driving along the beautiful shoreline when there was an enormous commotion heard just off the headland.

The Papal party rushed to see what it was, and upon approaching the scene, the Pope noticed in the water a hapless man wearing a TEXAS A&M football jersey, struggling frantically to free himself from the jaws of a 25-foot shark. At that moment a speedboat containing three men wearing Oklahoma Sooners' football jerseys roared into view from around the point. Immediately, one of the men took aim and fired a harpoon into the shark's ribs, immobilizing it instantly. The other two reached out and pulled the Texan from the water, and then, using long clubs, beat the shark to death.

They bundled the bleeding, semi-conscious man into

the boat along with the dead shark and were preparing for a hasty retreat when they heard frantic shouting from the shore. It was the Pope summoning them to the beach.

After they reached shore, the Pope praised them for the rescue and said, "I give you my blessing for your brave actions. I had heard that there was some bitter hatred between the people of Texas and Oklahoma, but now I have seen with my own eyes this is not true. I can see that your society is a truly enlightened example of true harmony and could serve as a model on which other states could follow." He blessed them all and drove off in a cloud of dust.

As he departed, the harpooner asked the others, "Who was that?"

"That was his Holiness the Pope," one answered. "He has a deep devotion to God and has access to God's wisdom."

"Well," the harpooner replied, "he don't know nothin' about shark fishin.' Is the bait were using holdin' up okay or do we need to get another one?"

Poof

One day three men were hiking and unexpectedly came upon a large raging, violent river. They needed to get to the other side but had no idea of how to do so.

The first man prayed to God, saying, "Please God, give me the strength to cross this river." Poof! God gave him big arms and strong legs, and after almost drowning a couple of times, he was able to swim across the river in about two hours.

Seeing this, the second man prayed to God, saying, "Please God, give me the strength and the tools to cross this river." Poof! God gave him a rowboat, and after almost capsizing the boat a couple of times, he was able to row across the river in about an hour.

The third man had seen how this worked out for the other two, so he also prayed to God, saying, "Please God, give me the strength and the tools...and the intelligence...to cross this river." And poof. God turned him into a woman.

She looked at the map, hiked upstream a couple of hundred yards, then walked across on the bridge.

Popular Song

The worst thing about a popular song is that it makes us all think we can sing.

Prepared Remarks

"Good evening, ladies and gentlemen. I'm pleased to be with you," said the speaker. He then paused, saying, "With that, I conclude my prepared remarks."

Priceless

My son swore he was going to give me something priceless for Christmas. He proved it. He didn't give me anything.

Professional Behavior

Doctors bury their mistakes. Lawyers hang them. But journalists put theirs on the front page.

Proper Grammar

I always make it a point to speak grammatically. Who knows? It might become popular again.

Bette Davis

Prosperity

Few of us can stand prosperity. Another man's, I mean.

Mark Twain

Psychiatrist

Patient: Doctor, doctor, I can't control my aggression.
Doctor: How long have you had this problem?
Patient: Who wants to know?

🌀 🌀 🌀 🌀 🌀

A new patient confided to the psychiatrist, "I'd better tell you before we begin...I suffer from marked suicidal tendencies."

"Very interesting," nodded the psychiatrist, with his best professional nod of the head. "Under the circumstances then, I'm quite sure you wouldn't mind paying the bill in advance."

🌀 🌀 🌀 🌀 🌀

Anybody who goes to see a psychiatrist ought to have his head examined.

🌀 🌀 🌀 🌀 🌀

All analysts are psychological, but some are more psycho than logical.

🌀 🌀 🌀 🌀 🌀

A patient lies down on the couch, and the shrink says, "Okay, tell me what you dreamed last night."

"I didn't dream."

"How can I help you if you don't do your homework?"

🌀 🌀 🌀 🌀 🌀

Brandy: I saw a psychiatrist today about my memory lapses.
Candy: Oh really? What did he say?
Brandy: He said I'd have to pay my bill in advance.

🌀 🌀 🌀 🌀 🌀

A doctor of psychology was doing his normal morning rounds when he entered a patient's room. He found Patient #1 sitting on the floor, pretending to saw a piece of wood in half. Patient #2 was hanging from the ceiling by his feet.

The doctor asked Patient #1 what he was doing. The patient replied, "Can't you see I'm sawing this piece of wood in half?" The doctor inquired of Patient #1 what Patient #2 was doing. Patient #1 replied, "Oh. He's my friend, but he's a little crazy. He thinks he's a light bulb." The doctor looks up and notices Patient #2's face is going all red.

The doctor asks Patient #1, "If he's your friend, you should get him down from there before he hurts himself!"

Patient #1 replies, "What! And work in the dark?"

🌀 🌀 🌀 🌀 🌀

Top Ten Signs a Therapist Is Approaching Burnout

10. You think of the peaceful park you like as "your private therapeutic milieu."

9. You realize that your floridly psychotic patient, who is picking invisible flowers out of midair, is probably having more fun in life than you are.

8. A grateful client, who thinks you walk on water, brings you a small gift, and you end up having to debrief your feelings of unworthiness with a colleague.

7. You are watching a rerun of *The Wizard of Oz*, and you start to categorize the types of delusions that Dorothy had.

6. Your best friend comes to you with severe relationship troubles, and you start trying to remember which cognitive behavioral technique has the most empirical validity for treating this problem.

5. You realize you actually have no friends, since they have all become just one big caseload.

4. A coworker asks how you are doing and you reply that you are a bit "internally preoccupied" and "not able to interact with peers" today.

3. Your spouse asks you to set the table and you tell them that it would be "countertherapeutic to your current goals" to do that.

2. You tell your teenage daughter she is not going to start dating boys because she is "in denial," "lacks insight." And her "emotions are not congruent with her chronological age."

And, the number one sign a therapist may be burning out....

1. You are dreading a trip to a large family holiday reunion because your family is "not therapeutically inclined."

Pun

Ron: That last joke of yours was two-thirds of a pun.
Don: How's that?
Ron: P.U.

A man who specialized in puns thought he had an outstanding chance of winning a pun contest run by his local newspaper. He sent the paper no fewer than ten different entries in the hope that one of them might win. Unfortunately, no pun in ten did.

Puns 'R' Us

- Marriage is the mourning after the knot before.
- Corduroy pillows are making headlines.
- Sea captains don't like crew cuts.
- Without geometry, life is pointless.
- When you dream in color, it's a pigment of your imagination.
- What's the definition of a will? (It's a dead giveaway.)
- In democracy, it's your vote that counts. In feudalism, it's your count that votes.

Purple

Q: What's purple and 5000 miles long?
A: The Grape Wall of China.

Push

My car works by push button. If the buttons don't work, I push.

Quack, Quack

A doctor and a lawyer were in a bitter dispute. The doctor said, "A little bird told me what kind of a lawyer you are—'cheep, cheep.'"

To which the lawyer retorted, "Well, a little duck told me what kind of a doctor you are."

Quick Learner

A young man applied for a government job. When asked what he could do, he said, "Nothing."

He got the job immediately. They wouldn't have to break him in!

Quits

Mary: So, you are expecting your seventh child! What do you think you'll call it?

Kerry: I think I'll call it quits!

Rabbit's Foot

A reporter interviewing a well-known scientist noticed that he was wearing a rabbit's foot on his key chain.

"Surely," said the reporter, "a man of science like you wouldn't believe in that old superstition."

"Certainly not," said the scientist, "but a friend of mine tells me it's supposed to bring you luck whether you believe in it or not."

Real Loser

He was a real loser. When his ship came in, he was waiting at the train station.

Real Sloppy

My son used to be real sloppy. He never tucked in his shirt. But my wife cured him. She sewed lace to the bottom of it!

Rubber Bands

Q: Do rubber bands lie?
A: No, they just stretch the truth.

Rush Hour

Why is the time of day with the slowest traffic called rush hour?

Senility Prayer

God, grant me the senility to forget the people
I never liked anyway, the good fortune to run into
the ones that I do, and the eyesight to tell
the difference.

Sign in an Art Gallery

We hung these pictures because we couldn't find the artists.

Sign on a Bakery Truck

What Foods These Morsels Be.

Silly Putty

My grandson is not too sharp. We bought him some Silly Putty to play with, and it outsmarted him.

Sinking

A woman goes fishing with her husband, and after about an hour she asks, "Do you have any more of those small plastic floats?"

"Why?"

"The one I'm using keeps sinking."

Sins

Sunday school teacher: Does anyone here know what we mean by sins of omission?

Student: Aren't those sins we should have committed, but didn't?

Sixty

I am pushing sixty. That is enough exercise for me.

Mark Twain

Skeleton in the Closet

A very large, old building was being torn down in Chicago to make room for a new skyscraper. Due to its proximity to other buildings, it could not be imploded and had to be dismantled floor by floor.

While working on the 49th floor, two construction workers found a skeleton in a small closet behind the elevator shaft. They decided that they should call the police.

When the police arrived, the workers directed them to

the closet and showed them the skeleton fully clothed and standing upright. They said, "This could be Jimmy Hoffa or somebody really important."

Two days went by and the construction workers couldn't stand it anymore—they had to know who they had found. They called the police and said, "We are the two guys who found the skeleton in the closet, and we want to know if it was Jimmy Hoffa or somebody important."

The police said, "It's not Jimmy Hoffa, but it *was* somebody kind of important."

"Well, who was it?"

"The 1956 National Blonde Hide-and-Seek Champion!"

Skintight Pants

We're constantly amazed at these young things with their fancy hairdos and skin tight pants. And the girls are even worse.

Skunk

A skunk in the bush is worth two in the hand.

Skydiving

I love to skydive. I jump out of a plane and try to land on a little black dot on the ground. But I have to remember to pull the rip cord so the black dot won't be me!

Sleep

Harris went to sleep at once. I hate a man who goes to sleep at once. There is a sort of indefinable something about it which is not exactly an insult and yet is an insolence.

Mark Twain

Slow

Uncle Dan claims he once dropped his watch from the roof, whereupon he carefully climbed down the ladder and caught the watch before it hit. "Of course," he says, "that watch always was 15 minutes slow."

Smart Cookie

An office manager was asking a female applicant if she had any unusual talents. She said she had won several prizes in crossword puzzle and slogan-writing contests.

"Sounds good," the manager told her, "but we want somebody who will be smart during office hours."

"Oh," said the applicant, "that *was* during office hours."

Smoke Alarm

I wouldn't say that my wife is a bad cook...but she does use a smoke alarm as a timer.

Smurf

If you choke a Smurf, what color does it turn?

Snake

Eve blamed the snake. The snake didn't have a leg to stand on.

Something to Live For

A woman yelled at her husband, "What do you mean you have nothing to live for? You have plenty to live for! The house isn't paid for, the car isn't paid for, the TV isn't paid for..."

Something to Offend Every College Football Fan

1. What does the average Texas A&M player get on his SATs? *Drool.*

2. How do you get a Colorado graduate off your porch? *Pay him for the pizza.*

3. Why is the Baylor football team like a possum? *Because they play dead at home and get killed on the road.*

4. What are the longest three years of an Oklahoma football player's life? *His freshman year.*

5. Where was O.J. headed in the white Bronco? *Lexington, Kentucky. He knew that the police would never look there for a Heisman Trophy winner.*

6. Why did Texas choose orange as their team color? *You can wear it for the game on Saturday, hunting on Sunday, and picking up trash along the highways the rest of the week.*

Son-Up

A mother who had just put her little boy to bed was heard to say as she shut the door and tiptoed down the hall, "This is one more day when I worked from son-up to son-down."

Speakers

Speakers fall into four categories:
  1. They don't have any notes, and the people have no idea how long they will speak.

2. Others put down on the podium in front of them each page of their sermon as they read it. These honest ones enable the audience to keep track of how much more is to come.

3. A few cheat by putting each sheet of notes under the others in their hand.

4. And, worst of all, some put down each sheet of notes as read and then horrify the audience by picking up the whole batch and reading off the other side.

Station

A janitor who worked in a railroad station decided to get married in a huge room on the upper floor of the station. So many friends and kinfolk showed up that their combined weight caused the building to collapse. Moral of the story: Never marry above your station.

St. Bernard

Dismayed by the size of the St. Bernard dog given him for his birthday, the little boy asked, "Is he for me, or am I for him?"

Stealth Bomber

If a stealth bomber crashes in a forest, will it make a noise?

Steamroller

A man was run over by a steamroller. His doctor told him to stay flat on his back.

@ @ @ @ @

A man was run over by a steamroller. He was in the hospital in rooms 38 to 44.

Sticky

Even when freshly washed and relieved of all obvious confections, children tend to be sticky.

Fran Lebowitz

Stock Market

I had some bad news in the market. My stock split. Unfortunately, so did my broker.

@ @ @ @ @

Let's face it, there's only one thing money can't buy—poverty! You need the stock market to get that.

@ @ @ @ @

Investing is easy. Buy a stock, and when it goes up, sell it. If it doesn't go up, don't buy it.

Will Rogers

Strike Out

The manager walks to the mound, ready to yank the pitcher. The pitcher protests, "I struck this guy out the last time."

"Yeah, but this is the same inning."

Sunday School

Son: Did you go to Sunday school every week when you were a boy?

Dad: I sure did, son.

Son: I'll bet it won't do me any good, either.

Super Glue

How come super glue doesn't stick to the tube?

Surprise

I asked the waitress, "What's the chef's surprise?"

She said, "He doesn't wash his hands."

Suspenders

A man was driving down the freeway, when suddenly he looked out his right window and saw a man on a bicycle, pedaling furiously as he passed him. The driver of the car stepped on the gas and went faster and passed the man on the bicycle. In just a moment, the man on the bicycle passed the car again. This time the driver of the car went even faster. Again the man on the bicycle passed the car.

Finally the driver of the car stopped. The man on the bicycle stopped by the right window. The driver of the car rolled down the window.

"Thank goodness you've stopped," said the man on the bicycle. "I had my suspenders caught in your back bumper."

Sweat

Why is it a businessman will go from his air-conditioned

house to his air-conditioned office in his air-conditioned car, then go to a health club and pay $50 an hour to sweat?

Synchronized

If one synchronized swimmer drowns, do the rest have to drown too?

Tech Support

Dear Tech Support,

Last year I upgraded from Boyfriend 5.0 to Husband 1.0 and noticed a slowdown in the overall performance, particularly in the flower and jewelry applications that had operated flawlessly under Boyfriend 5.0.

In addition, Husband 1.0 uninstalled many other valuable programs, such as Romance 9.5 and Personal Attention 6.5, but installed undesirable programs such as NFL 5.0 and NBA 3.0, and now Conversation 8.0 no longer runs and Housecleaning 2.6 simply crashes the system.

I've tried running Nagging 5.3 to fix these problems, but to no avail. What can I do?

> Signed,
> Desperate

Dear Desperate,

First of all, keep in mind that Boyfriend 5.0 is an entertainment package, but Husband 1.0 is an operating system. Try to enter the command: c:/I THOUGHT YOU LOVED ME and download Tears 6.2 to install Guilt 3.0.

If all works as designed, Husband 1.0 should then automatically run the applications Jewelry 2.0 and Flowers 3.5. But remember, overuse can cause Husband 1.0 to default to Grumpy Silence 2.5, a very bad program that will create Snoring Loudly.WAV files.

In summary, Husband 1.0 is a great program, but it does have a limited memory and cannot learn new applications quickly. You might consider buying additional software to improve memory and performance. I personally recommend Hot Food 3.0 and Sports Couch 7.7.

Good Luck,
Tech Support

Teenage Driver

I get about five miles to a gallon. My son gets the other twenty.

Teenager

When our phone rings, it's always for our daughter. When it isn't ringing, it's because she's talking on it. Sometimes when she's on our phone, the neighbors will come over and tell her she's wanted on their phone.

Art Frank

A teenager named Mary was in tears the other night. She had nothing to wear for her date. All her sweat shirts were in the wash.

Teeth Will Be Provided

"There will be weeping, wailing and gnashing of teeth among the wicked who pass on to the next world."

"What about those who haven't got any teeth?"

"Teeth will be provided."

Thirty Things I've Learned from My Children

1. There is no such thing as child-proofing your house.

2. If you spray hair spray on dust bunnies and run over them with roller blades, they can ignite.

3. A 3-year-old's voice is louder than 200 adults in a crowded restaurant.

4. If you hook a dog leash over a ceiling fan, the motor is not strong enough to rotate a 42-pound boy wearing Batman underwear and a Superman cape.

5. It is strong enough, however, to spread paint on all four walls of a 20-by-20-foot room.

6. Baseballs make marks on ceilings.

7. You should not throw baseballs up when the ceiling fan is on.

8. When using the ceiling fan as a bat, you have to throw the ball up a few times before you get a hit.

9. When you hear the toilet flush and the phrase "uh-oh," it's already too late.

10. Brake fluid mixed with Clorox makes smoke, and lots of it.

11. A six-year-old can start a fire with a flint rock even though a 36-year-old man says they can only do it in the movies.

12. A magnifying glass can start a fire even on an overcast day.

13. If you use a waterbed as home plate while wearing

baseball shoes it does not leak—it explodes.

14. A king size waterbed holds enough water to fill a 2000 square foot house 4 inches deep.

15. Legos will pass through the digestive tract of a four-year-old.

16. Duplos will not.

17. "Play-Doh" and "microwave" should never be used in the same sentence.

18. Super glue is forever.

19. No matter how much Jell-O you put in a swimming pool, you still can't walk on water.

20. Pool filters do not like Jell-O.

21. VCRs do not eject peanut butter and jelly sandwiches even though TV commercials show they do.

22. Garbage bags do not make good parachutes.

23. Marbles in gas tanks make lots of noise when driving.

24. You probably do not want to know what that odor is.

25. Plastic toys do not like ovens.

26. The fire department in Austin has at least a five-minute response time.

27. The spin cycle on the washing machine does not make earth worms dizzy.

28. It will, however, make cats dizzy.

29. Quiet does not necessarily mean you don't need to worry.

30. A good sense of humor will get you through most problems in life (unfortunately, mostly in retrospect).

Tie

A little boy took off his tie and put it into the offering plate. When his mother asked why, he replied: "The pastor told us to go give our ties and offerings."

Times Have Changed

1. Hardware used to refer to a store—not computer equipment.
2. Enter was a sign on a door, not a button on a computer keyboard, and chip was a piece of wood.
3. Fast food was what you ate during Lent.
4. Rock music, at one time, took place when grandma sang a lullaby in a rocking chair.

Tolerant

Always be tolerant of a person who disagrees with you. After all, he has a right to his ridiculous opinion.

Too Fast

A snail was crossing the road when he was run over by a tortoise. A policeman came along and asked him how it had happened. "I don't remember," said the snail. "It all happened so fast."

Too Late

"I beg your pardon for coming so late."

"My dear, no pardons are needed. You can never come too late."

Tuba

Fred: My next-door neighbors keep banging on the walls at all hours of the night.

Frank: Doesn't that bother you? How can you sleep?

Fred: I get plenty of sleep, but it interferes with my tuba practice.

Turn Around and Bend Over

If you kicked the person most responsible for your troubles, you wouldn't sit down for a week!

Turnips in Jail

I told my IRS auditor, "You can't get blood out of a turnip."

He answered, "No, but we can send the turnip to jail."

Turtle

Q: Where do you find a turtle without feet?

A: Exactly where you left him.

Twenty Miles an Hour

At the turn of the century, people were amazed when someone drove 20 miles an hour, and they still are.

Two

A student skydiver was being given instructions by the instructor: "You count to ten and just pull the rip cord."

The student said, "W-w-w-w-w-whhhatt w-w-w-was th-th-th-that n-n-num-m-mb-b-b-ber?"

The instructor said, "Two."

Two Ribbons

A man went into a pet store to buy a parrot. He noticed that one of the parrots had a red ribbon tied to one foot and a blue ribbon tied to the other foot.

Customer: Why does that parrot have ribbons tied to each of its feet?

Salesclerk: That is a very special parrot. He was trained to talk by pulling one of the ribbons. If you pull the red ribbon, the parrot will recite Psalm 23 from the Bible. If you pull the blue ribbon, the parrot will recite the Gettysburg Address by Abraham Lincoln.

Customer: What happens if you pull both ribbons at the same time?

At this point, the parrot screeched, "I will fall off my perch, stupid!"

Two Sides

There are always two sides to a question—if we aren't involved.

Two Sons

They have two children. The first is the president of a savings and loan, and the other one is in jail too.

Two Thousand Dollars

A patient walked into a doctor's office and was told he needed an operation. He asked, "What are you operating for?"

The doctor said, "Two thousand dollars."

The patient said, "No, I meant, what's the reason?"

The doctor said, "I told you—two thousand dollars!"

Ulcers

He doesn't have ulcers. He's just a carrier.

Undertakers

"My family follows the medical profession."

"Doctors?"

"No, undertakers!"

Unwind

What does a mummy do to unwind?

Value of Men and Women

- Women are compassionate, loving, and caring.
- Women cry when they are happy.
- Women are always doing little things to show they care.
- Women will stop at nothing to get what they think is best for their children—best school, best dress, best dentist.
- Women keep smiling when they are so tired that they can hardly stand up.

- Women know how to turn a simple meal into an occasion.

- Women know how to get the most for their money.

- Women know how to comfort a sick friend.

- Women bring joy and laughter to the world.

- Women know how to entertain children for hours on end.

- Women are honest and loyal.

- Women have a will of iron under that soft exterior.

- Women are easily brought to tears by injustice.

- Women know how to make a man feel like a king.

- Women make the world a much happier place to live in.

Now for the men:
- Men are good at moving heavy things and removing spiders.

Very Telling

"Mary told me that you told her the secret I told her not to tell you."

"Gee, and I told her not to tell you that I told her."

"Well, I wouldn't tell her I wouldn't tell you that she told, so don't tell her I told you."

Viola

Q: Why do viola players leave their cases on the dashboard of their car?

A: So they can park in handicapped zones.

🌀 🌀 🌀 🌀 🌀

Q: How can you tell if a viola is out of tune?

A: The bow is moving.

🌀 🌀 🌀 🌀 🌀

Q: What do a viola and a lawsuit have in common?

A: Everyone is happy when the case is closed.

Vote

While walking down the street one day, a female senator is tragically hit by a truck and dies. Her soul arrives in heaven and is met by Saint Peter at the entrance.

"Welcome to heaven," says Saint Peter. "Before you settle in, it seems there is a problem. We seldom see a high official around these parts, you see, so we're not sure what to do with you."

"No problem, just let me in," says the lady.

"Well, I'd like to, but I have orders from higher up. What we'll do is have you spend one day in hell and one in heaven. Then you can choose where to spend eternity."

"Really, I've made up my mind. I want to be in heaven," says the senator.

"I'm sorry, but we have our rules." And with that, Saint Peter escorts her to the elevator and she goes down to hell.

The doors open, and she finds herself in the middle of a green golf course.

In the distance is a club and standing in front of it are all her friends and other politicians who had worked with her.

Everyone is very happy. They run to greet her, hug her, and reminisce about the good times they had while getting rich at the expense of the people.

They play a friendly game of golf and proceed to dine on lobster and caviar.

Also present is the devil, who really is a very friendly guy who has a good time dancing and telling jokes. They are having such a good time that before she realizes it, it is time to go.

Everyone gives her a big hug and waves while the elevator rises.

The elevator goes all the way up, and the door reopens on heaven where Saint Peter is waiting for her.

"Now it's time to visit heaven." So 24 hours pass with the head of state joining a group of contented souls moving from cloud to cloud, playing the harp and singing. They have a good time, and before she realizes it, the 24 hours have gone by, and St. Peter returns.

"Well then, you've spent a day in hell and another in heaven. Now, choose the place where you want to spend eternity."

She reflects for a minute and then answers: "Well, I would never have said it, I mean heaven has been delightful, but I think I would be better off in hell."

So Saint Peter escorts her to the elevator, and she goes all the way down to hell.

Now, the doors of the elevator open, and she is in the middle of a barren land covered with waste and garbage. She sees all her friends, dressed in rags, picking up the trash and putting it in black bags.

The devil comes over to her and lays his arm on her neck.

"I don't understand," stammers the senator. "Yesterday I was here, and there was a golf course and club, and we ate lobster and caviar, danced, and had a great time. Now there is a wasteland full of garbage, and my friends look miserable."

The devil looks at her, smiles, and says, "Yesterday we were campaigning. Today, you voted for us!"

Waiter, Waiter

Customer: Waiter, what's this fly doing in my ice tea?
Waiter: Cooling off. It's very hot in the kitchen.

🌀 🌀 🌀 🌀 🌀

Customer: Waiter, what's this fly doing in my soup?
Waiter: It must have escaped from the salad.

🌀 🌀 🌀 🌀 🌀

Customer: Waiter, there's a fly in my soup.
Waiter: Let's hope for his sake that he didn't swallow any.

🌀 🌀 🌀 🌀 🌀

Customer: The service here is awful.
Waiter: How would you know? You haven't had any yet!

🌀 🌀 🌀 🌀 🌀

Customer: My juice is warm. I wanted it cold.
Waiter: If you wanted something cold, sir, you should have
ordered soup.

🌀 🌀 🌀 🌀 🌀

Customer: Hey, waiter! Over here! Didn't I say well done?
Waiter: Thank you, sir. I very seldom get a compliment.

🌀 🌀 🌀 🌀 🌀

Customer: Waiter, there's a fly in my soup.
Waiter: Now that fly knows good soup.

🌀 🌀 🌀 🌀 🌀

Customer: Waiter, there's dirt in my soup. What does this
mean?
Waiter: If you want your fortune told, go to a gypsy!

🌀 🌀 🌀 🌀 🌀

Customer: Waiter, there's a fly in my soup.
Waiter: What do you expect for a dollar—a monarch butter-
fly?

🌀 🌀 🌀 🌀 🌀

Customer: Waiter, I'll have the chef's salad.
Waiter: Really? Then what will the chef eat?

🌀 🌀 🌀 🌀 🌀

Epitaph for a dead waiter—God finally caught his eye.

George S. Kaufman

Wake Up

There is one phrase that is guaranteed to wake up an audience: "And now, in conclusion..."

Walking

A teenager kept insisting to his dad that he should have a car. Dad said, "You know your grades are down, you won't cut your hair, and your belief in God has gone to pot." He continued, "If you get your grades up, get your hair cut, and start reading the Bible, I'll think about it."

The boy protested, "But Dad, all the paintings show Jesus with long hair."

"I know," replied the father. "And if you actually read Scripture, you'll find that everywhere He went, He walked."

I had a bad accident, but the doctor told me that he'd have me walking again in no time. It was true. I had to sell my car to pay his bill.

Watching

All of the children at a Sunday School picnic were lined up for lunch. At the head of the table was a large basket of apples. The Sunday School teacher had made a note and posted it on the basket: *Take only one. God is watching.*

Moving further along the lunch line at the other end of

the table was a large pile of chocolate chip cookies. Next to the pile of cookies was a note written by one of the children in the class: *Take all you want. God is watching the apples.*

Weather

The prisoner, convicted of treason, is being marched to the firing squad in a downpour. He complains to his escort, "Look at this weather I have to walk through."

The escort says, "What are you complaining about? I have to walk back."

Weird Thing

The other day I saw a weird thing at a garage. The mechanic was wiping his hand on a rag when there was a brand new seat cover in front of him!

What Happened to Bessie?

This farmer has a cow he adores, but his pasture runs through some railroad land, and at the same hour daily, a train whizzes by. One day, the cow is missing, so the farmer sues the railroad. Before the case goes to the judge, the farmer agrees to settle for half. The railroad lawyer says, "You had us worried. You could have held out for it all."

The farmer says, "You had me worried too. The cow came home this morning."

Where Do I Live?

A young man walking down the street notices an elderly man sitting on a park bench, crying uncontrollably. Not wanting to intervene, but nonetheless concerned, the young man approaches the old man.

"Excuse me, sir, is everything all right?"

The old man looks up, tears filling his eyes. "Sonny," he says, "I am 90 years old. Last week I married the most beautiful woman in the world. She cooks for me. She cleans for me. She shops for me. She washes my cars for me. She basically does whatever I could possibly want or imagine."

"Oh," comments the young man, "that certainly doesn't seem bad at all. So, why are you crying?"

"Well," sobs the man. "I can't remember where I live!"

Where's Al?

Al and Greg go on a fishing trip. The first day, Al catches his limit. Greg gets nothing. Greg can't understand it. Maybe it was just dumb luck. The second day, Al can hardly get his line into the water before he snares a fish. All day long, Al keeps pulling them in. Greg decides to go out alone the third day.

He gets up at dawn, sneaks out, and is on the lake at sunrise. He drops his line into the water, feels a tug, pulls up the line, and there's a note attached to the hook: *Where's Al?*

Who Can Top This?

I didn't have any surgery this year, so it looks like I'll have to talk about my old one for another year.

Why?

Why do "overlook" and "oversee" mean opposite things?

Why God Made Moms

Answers to questions by elementary school children

1. Why did God make mothers?

"She's the only one who knows where the Scotch tape is."

"Mostly to clean the house."

"To help us out of there when we were getting born."

2. How did God make mothers?

"He used dirt, just like for the rest of us."

"Magic plus super powers and a lot of stirring."

"God made my mom just the same like he did me. He just used bigger parts."

3. What ingredients are mothers made of?

"God makes mothers out of clouds, angel hair, everything nice in the world, and one dab of mean."

"They had to get their start from men's bones. Then they mostly use string, I think."

4. Why did God give you your mother and not some other mom?

"We're related."

"God knew she would like me a lot more than other people's moms like me."

5. *What kind of little girl was your mom?*

"My mom has always been my mom and none of that other stuff."

"I don't know because I wasn't there, but my guess would be pretty bossy."

"They say she used to be nice."

6. *What did your mom need to know about your dad before she married him?*

"His last name."

"She had to know his background. Like is he a crook?"

"Does he make at least $800 a year? Did he say no to football and YES to chores?"

7. *Why did your mom marry your dad?*

"My dad makes the best spaghetti in the world. And Mom eats a lot."

"She got too old to do anything else with him."

"My grandma says that Mom didn't have her thinking cap on."

8. *Who's the boss at your house?*

"Mom doesn't want to be boss, but she has to because Dad's a goof ball."

"Mom. You can tell by room inspection. She sees the stuff under the bed."

"I guess Mom is, but only because she has a lot more to do than Dad."

9. *What's the difference between moms and dads?*

> "Moms work at work and work at home, and dads just go to work to work."

> "Moms know how to talk to teachers without scaring them."

> "Dads are taller and stronger, but moms have all the real power 'cause that's who you got to ask if you want to sleep over at your friend's."

> "Moms have magic: They make you feel better without medicine."

10. *What does your mom do in her spare time?*

> "Mothers don't do spare time."

> "To hear her tell it, she pays bills all day long."

11. *What would it take to make your mom perfect?*

> "On the inside she's already perfect. Outside, I think some kind of plastic surgery."

> "Diet. You know, her hair. I'd diet, maybe blue."

12. *If you could change one thing about your mom, what would it be?*

> "She has this weird thing about me keeping my room clean. I'd get rid of that."

> "I'd make my mom smarter. Then she would know it was my sister who did it and not me."

"I would like for her to get rid of those invisible eyes on the back of her head."

Why I Go to Church

A churchgoer wrote a letter to the editor of the newspaper and complained that it made no sense to go to church every Sunday. "I've gone for 30 years now," he wrote, "and in that time I have heard something like 3000 sermons. But for the life of me, I can't remember a single one of them. So I think I'm wasting my time and the pastors are wasting theirs by giving sermons at all."

This started a real controversy in the "Letters to the Editor" column, much to the delight of the editor. It went on for weeks until someone wrote this clincher: "I've been married for 30 years now. In that time my wife has cooked some 32,000 meals. But for the life of me, I cannot recall the entire menu for a single one of those meals. But I do know this: They all nourished me and gave me the strength I needed to do my work. If my wife had not given me these meals, I would be physically dead today. Likewise, if I had not gone to church for nourishment, I would be spiritually dead today!"

Willie Nelson

Q: What has 300 legs and seven teeth?
A: The front row at a Willie Nelson concert.

Windmill

A tourist saw his first country windmill and asked the farmer what it was. The farmer said, "It's an electric fan for blowing the flies off my cows."

Window

"On cable TV they have a weather channel—24 hours of weather. We had something like that where I grew up. We called it a window."

Wite-Out

Garth: I'm going to have to let that new secretary go.

Gertha: Don't you think she is learning word processing fast enough?

Garth: I don't think so. There is too much Wite-Out on the monitor screen!

Words of Woe

Blurting out the complete truth is considered adorable in the young, right smack up to the moment that the child says, "Mommy, is this the fat lady you can't stand?"

Judith Martin

Workaholics Anonymous

They have a new organization called Workaholics Anonymous. When you get the urge to put in an eight-hour day, you call them up and they send over two government workers to talk to you.

Worms

One of our neighbor's kids does bird impressions. He eats worms.

Worth $45,000

A man took a picture to an art shop for framing. At the

counter, he heard the woman in front of him tell the sales-clerk that she wanted a frame for a picture worth $45,000.

The clerk gasped and stammered that although the shop did not usually handle such expensive items, they would certainly do their best. The woman nodded and laid her son's college diploma on the counter.

Worthless

A sign on a dryer in a coin laundry reads: "This dryer is worthless." A sign on the next dryer reads: "This dryer is next to worthless."

Writing a Book

Novice to author: "I'm interested in writing a book. What's the best way to start writing?"

Author: "I suggest from left to right."

Wrong Way

An old man was driving on the freeway when his car phone rang. It was his wife. "Herman," she cried, "I just heard on the news that there's a car going the wrong way on 280. Please be careful."

"Good Golly," exclaimed Herman. "It's not just one car. It's hundreds of them!"

You Know You Are No Longer a Kid When...

1. Just one peanut butter and jelly sandwich doesn't do it any more.

2. Driving a car doesn't always sound like fun.

3. The average ten-year-old doesn't have a clue who Bo and Luke Duke are.

4. Being bad is no longer cool.

5. You have friends who have kids.

6. Saturday mornings are for sleeping.

7. You are taller than the slide at the McDonald's playland.

8. Your parents' jokes are now funny.

9. You have once said, "Whatch-you talkin' 'bout, Willis?"

10. You would rather wear your dirty clothes again 'cause Mom is not there to do your laundry anymore.

11. Two words: parachute pants.

12. Naps are good.

13. You have once deemed Space Invaders as "The best game ever."

14. When things go wrong, you can't just yell, "Do-over!"

15. The only thing in your cereal box is…cereal.

16. You actually buy scarves, gloves, and sunscreen.

17. Your idea of fun parties now include chips 'n' salsa and Snapple.

18. You leave concerts and ball games early to beat the crowd.

19. You *want* clothes for Christmas.

20. You don't want a Camaro because of the insurance premiums.

21. You remember when *Saturday Night Live* was funny.

22. You've bought an album on vinyl.

23. You remember seeing *Star Wars* when it first came out.

24. You look in the surveillance camera monitor at the convenience store, wonder who that guy is standing at the counter with the bald spot, and then realize it is a shot of you from behind.

You Might Be a Preacher If...

1. You've been asked, "What's so hard about preaching?"

2. Others wished they only worked one day a week for a week's pay!

3. If you have ever said, "I'm *never* going to be a preacher!"

4. You wear your new shoes to church, and someone comments, "We are paying you too much money!"

5. Women call up and say they want you to marry them.

6. You keep relating movies you've seen to sermon topics.

7. Your children are the worst kids in the church!

8. You name your bed "the Word." That way, you can tell everyone that you "stay in the Word."

9. You jiggle all the commode handles at the church before you leave.

10. Instead of being "ticked off," you get "grieved in your spirit."

11. You've ever dreamed you were preaching only to awaken and discover you were.

You're Not Well

A woman accompanied her husband to the doctor's office. After his checkup, the doctor called the wife into his office alone.

He said, "Your husband is suffering from a very serious disease, combined with horrible stress. If you don't do the following, your husband can die. Each morning, fix him a healthy breakfast. Be pleasant and make sure he is in a good mood. For lunch, fix him a nutritious meal. For dinner, prepare an especially nice meal for him. Don't burden him with chores. Don't discuss your stress or anything negative. This will probably make him feel worse.

"If you can do this for at least ten months to a year, I think your husband will regain his health completely."

On the way home, the husband asked his wife, "What did the doctor say to you?"

She replied, "You're going to die."

You're Somewhere

You're on the West Coast when...

- You make over $250,000 and still can't afford to buy your own house.

- The high school quarterback calls a time-out to answer his cell phone.

- The fastest part of your commute is going down your driveway.
- You know how to eat an artichoke.
- You drive to your neighborhood block party.

You're in New York when...
- You say "the city" and expect everyone to know you mean Manhattan.
- You have never been to the Statue of Liberty or the Empire State Building.
- You can get into a four-hour argument about how to get from Columbus Circle to Battery Park, but you can't find Wisconsin on a map.
- You think Central Park is "nature."
- You've worn out a car horn, but it's okay, because there's still two years left on the warranty.
- You think eye contact is an act of aggression.

You're in Alaska when...
- You only have four spices: salt, pepper, ketchup and Tabasco.
- Halloween costumes fit over parkas.
- You have more than one recipe for moose, and none of them involve chocolate.
- The four seasons are: almost winter, winter, still winter, and construction.

You're in the South when...
- You get a movie and bait in the same store.

- "Y'all" is singular and "all y'all" is plural.
- After ten years, you still hear, "You ain't from 'round here, are ya?"
- "He needed killin'" is a valid defense.

You're in Colorado when...
- You carry your $3,000 mountain bike atop your $500 car.
- You tell your husband to pick up Granola on his way home and he stops at the day care.
- A pass does not involve football or dating.
- The top of your head is bald, but you still have a ponytail.
- Your bridal registry is at four trendy outdoor stores, an herbalist, and a candle shop.

You're in the Midwest when...
- You've never met any celebrities, but the mayor knows your name.
- Your idea of a traffic jam is ten cars, waiting to pass a combine.
- You have had to switch from "heat" to "A/C" on the same day.
- You end sentences with a preposition: "Where's my coat at?" or "If you go to the mall, I wanna go with."
- When asked how your trip was to any exotic place, you say, "It was...diff'ernt."

You Stink

Angered at what he felt was a bad call, a pro player yelled at the referee, "You stink to high heaven."

The referee picked up the ball, walked off fifteen yards, and said, "Can you still smell me?"

Young

You'll always stay young if you live honestly, eat slowly, sleep sufficiently, work industriously, worship faithfully, and lie about your age.

Zebras

Two zebras stepped outside in the rain while Noah moved the animals aboard the Ark. One zebra says, "Why alphabetically?"

Zip

Old mailmen never die. They just lose their zip.

Other Books by Bob Phillips